Existentialism from Within

a *

The beginning and end of philosophy
is freedom.—SCHELLING

EXISTENTIALISM

from within

by

E. L. ALLEN

Ph.D. D.D.

GREENWOOD PRESS, PUBLISHERS
WESTPORT, CONNECTICUT

The Library of Congress has catalogued this publication as follows:

Library of Congress Cataloging in Publication Data

Allen, Edgar Leonard.
  Existentialism from within.

  Reprint of the 1953 ed.
  1. Existentialism. I. Title.
[B819.A6 1973]   192   72-7817
ISBN 0-8371-6526-1

$$B$$
$$819$$
$$A6.E9$$
$$1973$$

First published in 1953
by Routledge & Kegan Paul Ltd., London

Reprinted with the permission
of Routledge & Kegan Paul Ltd.

First Greenwood Reprinting 1973

Library of Congress Catalogue Card Number 72-7817

ISBN 0-8371-6526-1

Printed in the United States of America

To the abiding memory of
Frank Granger
who, after many years,
is still a presence

Preface

Of the various books on Existentialism in English known to me, most appear to be based on inadequate knowledge and to be mistaken in judgment. There is room therefore for a presentation that is sympathetic and seeks to bring out what is of permanent value in this new movement.

The impulse to the production of this book was given by an invitation to deliver two lectures on Existentialism at an Easter Vacation Course in Philosophy under the auspices of the University of London's Institute of Education in 1951. But the material has undergone so thorough a revision that scarcely anything remains of the original lectures.

Acknowledgment is hereby made to the following publishers for permission to quote from the books mentioned: Geo. Allen & Unwin, Ltd. (Husserl's *Ideas*), Victor Gollancz, Ltd. (Jaspers's *Way to Wisdom*), Basil Blackwell (Robbio's *Philosophy of Decadentism*), Harvill Press, Ltd. (Marcel's *The Philosophy of Existence* and *The Mystery of Being*),

Preface

Methuen & Co. Ltd. (Sartre's *Existentialism and Humanism*), Oxford University Press (Kierkegaard's *Concept of Dread*), the same with Princeton University Press (Kierkegaard's *Training in Christianity*).

E. L. ALLEN

King's College
Newcastle upon Tyne

Contents

1. Introduction

IN the English-speaking countries, existentialism has yet to win anything like full recognition in academic circles, though on the Continent it has long since established itself. But where it is not yet known as a serious philosophy it commands interest as one of the very latest literary fashions. In this respect, its position is similar to that of psycho-analysis a generation ago. The novels of Sartre are read by many who do not grasp the moral purpose behind the deliberately nauseating account he gives of human life in our great cities. His plays delight a few, intrigue more, and, one may suspect, puzzle most of those who go to see them. A novelist like Camus distresses one by his portrait of *The Outsider* and then goes on to write *The Plague* as a *credo* of atheist humanism. It is clear that something new is abroad, something that seems to threaten traditional values in a more overt way than anything in literature since Nietzsche, and yet that gives signs, as indeed he did, of offering new values of its own making.

Perhaps indeed existentialism should not be treated as a philosophy. Certainly, Kierkegaard—and of him we shall have much more to say in the sequel—never aspired to be numbered among the philosophers. He dreaded the day when he would be incorporated into text-books and got up for examination purposes. There are indications that what he feared is coming to pass. The German thinkers whom he has influenced tend, as might have been expected, to conform to traditional patterns of presentation. It was reserved for Jaspers, however, to build a system out of the insight that truth can never be a system—and to succeed amazingly in doing so. Heidegger's *Sein und Zeit* 1ste *Hälfte* is surely one of the most obscure books ever written, and a distinguished Chinese professor of philosophy who was in Germany when it appeared assured me that the explanation of its popularity could lie only in its unintelligibility. In *L'Être et le Néant* the existentialism of Sartre takes on immense proportions and even the natural lucidity of the French language yields at times to the subtlety of his argument, so that few who attempt to expound him can be confident of their success.

Like Sartre, Marcel has used both media of expression, the formal philosophical discussion and the novel or play. Even he, however, warns us at the beginning of his Gifford Lectures that what follows will be less adequate as an expression of his thought than his dramas have been.[1] And this is intelligible when we remember what existentialism is. It cannot be presented as other philosophies have been, because one of its major contributions to philosophy is the insistence that, as it has been put, the *how* of truth is as important

[1] *The Mystery of Being*, I (1950), 22.

2

Introduction

as the *what*, in other words, that concrete truth cannot be expressed in the language appropriate to abstract truths. What this means will be seen better if I hazard a definition of existentialism in a sentence. *Existentialism is an attempt at philosophizing from the standpoint of the actor instead of, as has been customary, from that of the spectator.*[1]

(*a*)

What of the pedigree of this new movement? We can carry its ancestry far back, as far back at any rate as to Augustine, in whose *Confessions* we find just that encounter of the individual with his mortal destiny, dread, anguish, and despair, with which the existentialists of today familiarize us. Why indeed should we stop there? We might well return to Socrates. For does not the closing section of the *Apology* thrill us as we read it centuries later by its existentialist attitude to death? 'I do not know,' he says, 'what lies in the beyond, but I go forward with courage and hope, and I shall find out in good time.' The arguments in the *Phaedo* for the immortality of the soul may lack cogency as arguments, but they have a deeper value. They are the expressions of the faith in which Socrates meets death, the faith of one who has so lived that he can welcome it as the consummation of all that he has desired and striven after.

[1] Julien Benda describes existentialism as a revolt of life against the idea and thought. (*Tradition de l'existentialisme*, 1947, 11ff.) For Emmanuel Mounier it is 'a reaction of the philosophy of man against the excesses of the philosophy of ideas and the philosophy of things'. (*Existentialist Philosophies*, 1948, 2.) The first judgment is that of a hostile critic, the second that of a friend.

Or we might return to the Bible. One of the greatest services rendered by Kierkegaard was that he enriched philosophy with themes and categories taken originally from the Bible. The conception of man that governs the Old Testament finds its echoes in Jaspers and Marcel,[1] while a recent study of the Pauline anthropology is frankly existentialist in its approach.[2] The work of Rudolf Bultmann has shown how it is possible to illuminate the New Testament by the use of categories derived from it in the first instance, though they have been recast philosophically in the course of transition. This is not, as its critics have sometimes supposed, the reading back into the Bible of present-day ideas; those ideas have only become current among us because they were preserved for us within the Christian tradition. What is new is their acceptance into philosophy.

We might name Pascal as a kindred soul to Kierkegaard, and at once we recognize the common Christian inspiration. One great difference between the two men was that the Frenchman's early devotion to mathematics gave him a clarity and directness of approach wanting in the Dane. I would myself say that the influence of Kant has not been given its due weight. Did he not establish the sharp distinction between the scientific ordering of the data of sense-experience that yields knowledge and that encounter with the noumenal which is the privilege of freedom and the moral

Cf. Eichrodt: *Man in the Old Testament* (1951); Crespy: *Le problème d'une anthropologie théologique* (1950).
[2] Mehl-Koehnlein: *L'homme selon l'apôtre Paul* (1951).

Introduction

consciousness? Where Kant is defective may be seen from his so-called moral argument for God's existence. This is rather belief in God than faith in him, the assumption of his existence and not personal commitment to him. Or, the relation between Kant and existentialism might be stated in another way. Kant showed the central importance of the subject for knowledge; it is we who confer significance on what is given in sensation. His cosmos is anthropocentric in that respect. But the centre is occupied by man as a rational being, by consciousness-in-general. For Heidegger and the existentialists generally this place is taken by man as the living, growing being that each of us actually is with his freedom and responsibility, his guilt and mortality.

Three others deserve at least a passing mention. The entry on the title-page of this book is clear evidence that Schelling may not be overlooked. We know that Marcel was influenced by him in his earliest phase.[1] Even more important is the fact that Kierkegaard attended his lectures in Berlin and at first was carried away with enthusiasm for him. 'I have put all my hopes in Schelling', he writes. Soon, to be sure, he had ceased to learn from him and could complain to his brother that 'Schelling drivels on quite intolerably'.[2] There are passages in Schelling's works that set out in

---

[1] 'As against this (the philosophy of Spinoza) I seemed to discern, at the end of the immense journey travelled by Schelling, a light which perhaps might help me one day to discover my own path.' Marcel: *The Philosophy of Existence* (1948), 78. In the same autobiographical essay, he tells us that his main position was reached before he had any knowledge of Kierkegaard.

[2] *The Journals* (1938), 102, 104.

5

advance the main positions reached subsequently by the existentialists. Thus, he can say that 'man's being is essentially *his own deed*'.[1] The notion of a choice of oneself, so prominent in Kierkegaard, was clearly derived by him from Schelling. The glorification of freedom in Schelling is such that he identifies it with the Abyss out of which God emerges; it is a dynamic creative principle, a longing that gives birth to light or reason. In this he is followed by Berdyaev. One of the most valuable of recent studies of Schelling deliberately resorts to the terminology of existentialism. His aim, we are told, was 'to show the reality, the factual existence, which idealism failed to account for, and to construct a positive science of such existence'.[2]

In the final phase of his life, Kierkegaard was attracted to Schopenhauer, and it is difficult not to believe that his pessimism and his final revolt against the Church owed something to that influence. Indeed, he suggested that every Danish theological student would do well to take a dose of Schopenhauer's ethics as an antidote to the mediocre, worldly-minded Christianity of the day.[3] But Schopenhauer himself was lacking in the asceticism he preached; there was nothing of the existentialist self-commitment in him.

In France, Maine de Biran must be mentioned in any attempt to trace the origins of contemporary

[1] *Of Human Freedom*, trans. Jas. Gutmann (1936), 63.

[2] Schelling: *The Ages of the World*, trans. Bolman (1942), 65. So Arthur O. Lovejoy finds the significance of Schelling to lie in the 'introduction of a radical evolutionism into metaphysics and theology'. (*The Great Chain of Being*, 1936, 325. Cf. the importance for Kierkegaard of God as *becoming* (*Philosophical Fragments, passim*).

[3] *The Journals*, 506f.

6

Introduction

existentialism. Mounier, for example, expressly includes him in the genealogical tree he constructs.[1] His philosophy was voluntarist and personalist, in open reaction against the materialism of the mid-nineteenth century.[2]

But it is with Kierkegaard that we must principally be concerned.

(b)

I shall consider Kierkegaard here not for his own sake, but solely for the initial impetus he gave to the contemporary movement. The reader who wishes for more extensive information should have no difficulty in finding it elsewhere.

Kierkegaard himself stated his own conclusions in definite opposition to those of Hegel. It has been claimed that he misunderstood Hegel and so did him grave injustice.[3] That may well be so, but it is not our immediate concern. For what roused Kierkegaard's ire was not so much the philosophy of Hegel itself as its application to theology. It seemed to him that Hegel had substituted the development of the Idea for those historical facts that are life and death to Christianity. Kierkegaard objected, too, to the claim that the standpoint of speculation represents an advance upon that of faith. This was indeed a return to the Gnosticism against which the Church had to contend in the early

[1] Op. cit., 3. See Cresson: Maine de Biran (1950).
[2] Other names that might be mentioned are those of Josiah Royce, Max Scheler, Max Weber, Wilhelm Dilthey (see Hodges: Wilhelm Dilthey An Introduction, 1944, 107f.), and Henri Bergson.
[3] Ramsey: 'Existenz and the Existence of God: A Study of Kierkegaard and Hegel' in The Journal of Religion (1948), 157ff.

7

centuries. Hegel aspired to 'mediate' everything, to find a place for it in his all-embracing system. His watchword was *Both-And*, whereas life works with *Either-Or*. Hegel, so Kierkegaard declared with fine scorn, sits in a box in the world-theatre, watching and criticizing the play of history. Fool! docs he not know that there is only one box and that is reserved for God, while he himself is on the stage with the rest of us, required to play his part?[1] In other words, the truth of a situation is only grasped when it is seen from within, by those who are living through it.

It follows from this that truth is subjective and brings responsibility with it. The first point may be illustrated by a rather amusing story Kierkegaard tells. A patient escapes from a lunatic asylum and, in order to escape detection, confines himself in conversation to unimpeachably objective statements. So he says to everyone he meets, 'The earth is round.' He has not done this many times when he is identified as an escaped lunatic and sent back whence he came.[2] Why? Is it then not true that the earth is round? Of course it is, but true for anybody and everybody, for Kant's consciousness-in-general, not for this man personally in his concrete situation.

What of truth as responsibility? Kierkegaard said that many philosophers are like a man who built a magnificent palace and then went to live in a hovel somewhere on the grounds. They construct systems of exalted idealism and live all the while the narrow,

[1] *Unscientific Postscript* (1941), 141.
[2] *Ibid.*, 174.

8

Introduction

comfortable lives of the middle class.[1] So Schopenhauer preached universal pity and in practice was callous and selfish. Against all such perversions it must be maintained that only that on which we are prepared to act is really true for us. Here, Kierkegaard insisted, is one of the sins of the Church. How cuttingly he satirizes the theological student, for example, who can discourse eloquently on the self-sacrifice of Christ—in the hope of attracting the attention of a wealthy patron who can introduce him to a comfortable living where he can marry and settle down! Or the bishop who, with a row of orders on his chest, bids us renounce for Christ's sake the pomp and vanity of this world! All this is so much self-deception. One should be sincere as a man, not merely consistent as a thinker. Truth calls for commitment.

To the type of thinking that is thus personal and issues in commitment Kierkegaard gives the name of 'existential'. The term goes back ultimately to the scholastic distinction between essence and existence. 'Essence is what a being is. Existence is the act by which a being is.'[2] The essence of a thing is the totality of its distinctive characteristics. This marks it off from all other things. But it contains no guarantee that the thing actually exists. The unicorn can be defined by the characteristics that separate it from all other objects of thought; but it is still no more than an object of thought. If one actually met a unicorn, one would then

[1] *The Journals*, 156.
[2] Olgiati-Zybura: *The Key to the Study of St. Thomas*, 43; quoted in M. C. D'Arcy: *Thomas Aquinas* (1933), 108.

9

know that it existed. So that it is only when one speaks in terms of existence that one enters the actual world; apart from this, one is only in the realm of what is possible and may be thought. To think existentially is therefore to come to grips with the human situation as one in which we are actually involved. ·

The existential thinker is thus the actual, living, striving person whose thought is embedded in his life, is indeed part of the process of living. What happens to him is never merely something to be investigated, it is something with which he is concerned. More important still, he is continually concerned about himself. For the human situation is an intensely precarious one. The existential thinker makes no pretence to disinterested knowledge. He has no time for the general problem of the immortality of the soul, he is so preoccupied with the fateful possibility and certainty of his own death. That prospect colours all his life. He cannot afford to postpone problems till he has the time to grapple with them, not at any rate the really major problems. He must find some tentative solution to them such as will enable him to live through the suffering of the present hour and accept responsibility for its decisions. He cannot, in these matters, think of himself as contributing to a body of knowledge that will accumulate through the generations, he must round off his life here and now, give it a meaning while he still has the opportunity, for tomorrow may well be too late. This point of view is clearly not the scientific one, not even the psychological; it is ethical through and through.

Introduction

(c)

There will be opportunity in what follows to point out from time to time where later thinkers have contracted an indebtedness to Kierkegaard beyond what has been indicated thus far. But it may be of value to mention at this stage three defects in his thinking, three problems that he left to his successors. These are the problems of community, commitment, and objectivity.

(i) While we today tend to look back upon the nineteenth century as a time of rampant individualism, Kierkegaard was conscious rather of the tyranny of the mass-mind. In this he has the support of Ibsen and Nietzsche. The result is that he felt himself called to champion the individual against the mass. The murder of Coriolanus in Shakespeare's play of that name appealed to him as a symbol of contemporary flight from responsibility. Who killed Coriolanus? No one did, it was the act of a crowd in which the individual was submerged, so that he could do unashamedly what conscience would not have allowed him to do by himself. True, Kierkegaard's individualism was of a religious order, he wanted to bring each man into relation to God. But, while he was not unaware that such a personal meeting with God ought to be at the same time the entry into community with one's fellows, he never did justice to this. Hence his own inability to marry and his negative attitude to the Church. It was the task of later thinkers to effect the necessary distinctions between individuality and personality on the one hand and society and community on the other. While the individual is correlated with society, which may be no more than an organization imposed upon those who are in no way inwardly related, the person comes to himself only within community and its mutual giving and receiving.

(ii) As has just been indicated, it was one of the saddest features in the unhappy life of Kierkegaard that he who preached commitment was unable to commit himself. When he did take the decisive step of declaring himself by open attack upon the Church, there was more of passion than of genuine commitment in this. While he could praise the married estate, he thought of himself as the exceptional individual, called to a relation to God that kept him from binding himself to his fellows. Politically, he was conservative and capable only of a superficial judgment on the work of Grundtvig and the Danish national awakening of the time. He thought of political life as the sphere of authority, not as a call to active participation by the Christian citizen. It is the merit of Sartre that he grappled with this problem. As will be seen in due course, however negative Sartre's version of existentialism is in some important respects, it is at least wholly free from escapism. He understands commitment as attachment to tasks and causes in one's society; the philosopher must not shrink from the dust and heat even of political conflict. Indeed, there are those who would criticize his views on literature as threatening to reduce it to propaganda. His *Portrait of the Anti-Semite* and *The Respectable Prostitute* leave no doubt where he would have the reader stand on two major social issues.

(iii) Kierkegaard's emphasis on the subjectivity of truth was, as he himself well knew, one-sided. It was meant as a protest against the tyranny of science, which, he remarks, has come to take the place of religion for many.[1] But he goes on virtually to deprive science of any value. 'It is incredible that a man who has thought infinitely about himself as a spirit could think of choosing natural science (with empirical material) as his life's work and aim.'[2] Certainty resides only in ethics and religion; science therefore is unworthy of serious interest. He seems to be unaware that objective truth, albeit of a different order, is as necessary to ethics and religion as to natural science. There is as much need to be on one's guard against wishful thinking in the one case as in the other. I need to be sure that the truth to which I commit myself is quite independent of my act of commitment. Religious faith is an insight into what *is*, the prophet bows under the constraint of a reality that takes no cognizance of his own wishes, in the hour of moral decision a man cries

> It fortifies my soul to know
> That, though I perish, truth is so.

When the characters in Marcel's dramas ask the question: 'What am I?' their whole effort is directed towards an objective truth. While Heidegger has been

[1] *The Journals*, 363.
[2] *Op. cit.*, 185.

accused of recognizing only a relative and man-made truth, Jaspers has shown, by his insistence on the correlation of existence and Transcendence, how the truth that wins me personally is at the same time the truth that is sovereignly independent of me. Once this position has been established, it is possible to take with him the further step of seeing in the structures of objective truth the necessary media for communication between selves. So, I can only give myself to my neighbour in our concrete situation because there is a language common to us both and applicable to all situations.

(d)

If what has been said of existentialism so far is at all accurate, it will be clear that it cannot have come about by any natural development within philosophy. It must be rooted, as for it all human thinking is, in a concrete historical situation. The term 'philosophy of crisis' has been used for it, and used legitimately.[1] This at once invites comparison with the 'theology of crisis', associated with the names of Barth and Brunner. Both can be understood only as they are seen within their historical setting. The German collapse and the Russian revolution shattered the traditional framework within which these people had lived hitherto. Even in more favoured lands, millions of men had experiences that compelled them to accept responsibility and to face death. So they were introduced to the essential

[1] Bobbio: *The Philosophy of Decadentism* (1948), 1ff. It should be added that I regard this book as highly misleading.

14

Introduction

concern of existentialism, which is with the poignant uncertainty and arduous freedom characteristic of our life in this world, with man not as a rational being merely, but with man as a creature subject to finitude, torn with anxiety, and stabbed awake to the predicament of his mortality.

Nevertheless, it would be a grave error to dismiss existentialism as a mere post-war phenomenon, a nightmare of defeated peoples that will be shaken off when they awake to a happier day. This would indeed be to beg the question from the outset. For the existentialist would say that nothing human ever is a product of conditions. Man exists as a being in situations, and his situation is always something more than the sum of his circumstances. He is himself an all-important factor in his situation, so that in the last resort he is not determined by it but determines it. If he allows it to determine him, that is because he has freely surrendered the exercise of his freedom, so that the principle of self-determination still holds good. The most that circumstances can do is to restrict the possibilities of action, to present us with alternatives between which we must choose. The post-war world is not our fate, it is a challenge to us, and we determine by our response to that challenge whether it will be the last hour of Western man or the beginning of a new phase in his history. Existentialism, I would grant, is rooted in the post-war situation; but I would insist that it transcends it.

Before this introductory chapter is concluded, some notice must be taken of one other influence, one this

Introduction

time of quite academic character. The most important of Sartre's philosophical writings has as its sub-title: 'an essay in phenomenological ontology'. It thereby proclaims its derivation from the school of Husserl and at the same time its breach with this. Husserl's phenomenology is extremely difficult to summarize, particularly as it passed through several phases and was, in his view, misunderstood by almost all its interpreters. I will simply say here that it was an attempt to find a fresh starting-point for philosophy by getting behind the common-sense and scientific views of the world and attaining to an immediate insight. In his *Ideas* and the article on Phenomenology contributed to the 14th edition of the *Encyclopaedia Britannica* he distinguishes between fact and essence, between objects or psychic processes as actual occurrences and the patterns or essences that confer upon these occurrences their specific characters. The concern of phenomenology is with the latter. To reach them it employs what it calls 'phenomenological reduction', by which the everyday experience of the world and ourselves as real is held in suspense, is as it were put in brackets. It is neither denied nor affirmed, attention being directed elsewhere. We thus occupy a transcendental standpoint, as Kant would have called it. What then remains over on the objective side (this of course includes consciousness also when consciousness is studied) is not the individual fact, but an ideal object or essence, the colour as such and not this particular colour, the volition as such and not this or that volition. While Husserl dreamed of a universal philosophy to be reached in this way, his

16

Introduction

own main work was done in what he called phenomenological psychology. Once the transcendental
standpoint has been reached, the question demands to
be answered: 'What can remain over when the whole
world is bracketed, including ourselves and all our
thinking?' In the effort to answer this, we arrive at 'a
new region of Being, the distinctive character of which
has not yet been defined, a region of individual Being'.
This is the region of pure consciousness, of consciousness in general, as opposed to my consciousness and
yours. The fundamental structure of consciousness in
this sense is seen on investigation to be intentionality,
and intentionality is always directed upon an object.
The object may belong to what is not consciousness or
to consciousness itself. Perception or intuition has a
self-certainty in the second case that is lacking in the
first. Hence a restatement of the Cartesian *Cogito ergo
sum* becomes possible.

'If reflective apprehension is directed to my
experience, I apprehend an absolute Self whose existence (*Dasein*) is, in principle, undeniable, that is, the
insight that it does not exist is, in principle, impossible;
it would be nonsense to maintain the possibility of an
experience *given in such a way not* truly existing. The
stream of experience which is mine, that, namely, of
the one who is thinking, may be to ever so great an
extent uncomprehended, unknown in its past and
future reaches, yet as soon as I glance towards the
flowing life and into the real present it flows through,
and in so doing grasp myself as the pure subject of this
life (what that means will expressly concern us at a

17

later stage), I say forthwith and because I must: *I am*, this life is, I live: *cogito*.'[1]

From this it is then deduced that 'the pure Ego and its personal life' stand as necessary and indubitable over against a world that is contingent and has only 'presumptive reality'. 'All corporeally given thing-like entities can also not be, no corporeally given experiencing can also not be.'[2] The Cartesian dualism returns in a new form.

The reader is asked to keep these passages from Husserl in mind when he reads the exposition of Sartre, and he will recognize at once the source of the distinction between the two forms of Being, Being-in-itself and Being-for-itself, together with the whole discussion on necessity and contingency.

The radically new step taken, first by Heidegger and then by Sartre, is the deliberate application of Husserl's method to the one region from which it was explicitly excluded by him, that of Being. They seek to win an insight into the structures of Being and to set out what they have seen. Of course, in this application the method itself underwent such a change that the originator refused to recognize it as his.[2] But they took over from him the essential feature of his method, the resolute effort to thrust through the thicket of 'natural knowledge' and accepted ideas to a first-hand encounter with what enters into experience.

[1] *Ideas* (1931), 112, 143, 145. I have not always reproduced the italics used in the original.
[2] A. de Waehlens: *La Philosophie de Martin Heidegger* (1942), 21.

2. The Challenge of Death [1]

O F Heidegger's close connection with Husserl there can be no doubt. He was not only a student under him at Freiburg but also became his successor. But his earliest work was done on medieval philosophy,[2] and this concern with Christianity in its Catholic form has deeply coloured his thought ever since. He is one of those modern thinkers who may deny God but cannot be indifferent to him. That, as we shall see, is even more true of Sartre. But Heidegger's concern is with something much older and more fundamental than the logic of Duns Scotus or Aristotle. He deliberately returns beyond Plato to the earliest Greek thinkers. He insists that the problem with which he is concerned is not that of existence but that of Being, that he belongs with Parmenides rather than with Kierkegaard. He refuses to be classed along with Jaspers.

(a)

The first page of *Sein und Zeit* carries a quotation from Plato that makes it clear what the author's prim-

[1] Throughout this chapter I am greatly indebted to A. de Waehlens: *La Philosophie de Martin Heidegger* (1942).
[2] *Die Kategorien— und Bedeutungslehre des Duns Scotus* (1916).

ary concern is.[1] Indeed, he had shown as much in his inaugural lecture under the title *What is Metaphysics?* Here he concentrates on a particular problem, that of the Nothing. To many, of course, this will seem at once a spurious problem, due, as we are told nowadays, to a mistaken use of language. Since there are many possible statements that negate—such as 'This is not sweet', 'he did not come', 'they do not like me', we fall into the error of supposing that there is some 'nothing' or 'nought' that must somehow exist, since otherwise it could not be predicated in these different ways. But there is nothing of the kind: the Nothing is merely an abstraction from the various instances of negation: it has no substance of its own, but is parasitical upon what is denied in each case. Heidegger does not agree. For him there is an actual experience of the Nothing. It is inseparably bound up with Being. The experience that attests this is that of dread.

Here Heidegger draws upon Kierkegaard, who devoted one of his most remarkable books to an analysis of the phenomenon of dread and an account of it as the condition making sin possible.[2] This dread, Kierkegaard tells us, is correlated with nothing. He asks the question: 'What effect does nothing produce?' and answers that 'it begets dread'.[3] But while he thus borrows from Kierkegaard his starting-point, his interest thereafter is in the Nothing itself and not in the

---

[1] 'It is clear that you knew all along what you mean when you use the expression "being", while we formerly thought we understood what it meant, but are now perplexed by it.' *Sophistes*, 244a.
[2] *The Concept of Dread.*
[3] *Ibid.*, 38.

dread that makes us aware of it. When we are face to face with the Nothing we are dreadfully aware of the peril overhanging all that is, it seems to be slipping away from us into the void yet at the same time to attract and claim us. If I may hazard an analogy Heidegger does not himself use, at the risk of misinterpreting him, it is as when we find our consciousness of the value of something enhanced by a sudden realization of how precarious our possession of it is. Only, of course, at the level of experience that Heidegger is describing, what is brought home sharply to us is not that something is so, but simply that it *is*.

It may be objected that dread is abnormal, pathological even, and that it is unwise to infer anything from it. While granting its exceptional character, Heidegger would say that it is a pointer to something deeper and more permanent. We are aware of what is as haunted by the possibility of falling into the Nothing, and it is just this awareness that gives to it its arresting and poignant character. 'Nothing is that which makes the revelation of what-is as such possible for our human existence.'[1] In other words, there is no such thing as a science of being. Being is apprehended existentially or not at all; we are aware of it as a wonder over against the awful possibility of Nothing. The question: 'Why is there anything at all and not rather nothing?' was not meant as a parallel to, for example, the question: 'Why is there a bus-station here and not rather an empty space?' It does not call for an explanation, it evokes awe and a sense of wonder.

[1] *Existence and Being* (1949), 370. 'Existence' renders *Dasein* in the original.

The Challenge of Death

The value of Heidegger's thesis in this lecture is that it offers a reinstatement of wonder as the basic and original philosophical attitude. We may not take anything for granted, least of all ourself and our own life. The question: 'Why am I here at all?' is a genuine one, as an expression of awe and gratitude. It leads on to the consciousness that life is a trust, that, as Jaspers would put it, I have been given to myself. It is therefore an essentially religious attitude that Heidegger seeks to evoke, whether or not he himself would describe it as such.

Further, is there a suggestion here as to how we may understand existentially the Christian doctrine of *creatio e nihilo*? Heidegger himself says that 'every being, so far as it is a being, is made out of nothing'.[1] By this he does not mean, nor does the Christian doctrine mean, that there was a pre-existent nothing out of which all things were made. From the Christian point of view, may we not say that God's creative power is exercised continually in the maintenance of what is against the threat of the Nothing? We interpret the wonder before Being that has been spoken of as wonder before God; that is the final explanation of its awe-inspiring and 'numinous' quality.[2]

In *Sein und Zeit* we have a different approach to the

---

[1] *Op. cit.*, 377.

[2] 'The Christian view takes the position that non-being is everywhere present as the Nothing out of which all is created, as appearance and vanity, as sin, as sensuousness divorced from the spirit, as the temporal forgotten by eternity; wherefore the whole point is to do away with it and get being in its stead.' Kierkegaard: *The Concept of Dread*, 74. Should one seek the explanation of Karl Barth's account of sin in his *Kirchliche Dogmatik*, III, with its apparent Neo-Platonism, along these lines?

problem—or, as we should call it with Marcel—the mystery of Being. The suggestion here is that an abstract treatment of the theme would be quite out of place and is rendered unnecessary by the fact that we have a privileged instance of Being within our reach. Indeed, *we* are this. We know ourselves from within as nothing else can ever be known to us. Further, to know ourselves is part of what we are. Man is the point at which Being, so to speak, comes to light, finds expression. While everything else falls within Being, man alone is aware of this. Some apprehension of Being is therefore an integral part of his being; the obligation to know himself is laid upon him by the simple fact of being human. Or, to say the same thing in other words, man can only think and speak of Being as he bears in mind that he is involved in it; to forget this is to think and speak of something else. Man has to find the language in which Being can utter itself, and what Heidegger calls his 'fundamental ontology' is an effort in this direction.

Now we are able to see why he does not admit that he should be associated with Kierkegaard. He distinguishes between the *existential* approach, which is his own, and the *existentiel*, which derives from Kierkegaard and is represented today by Jaspers.[1] He defines *Existenz* as 'the self's possibility, to be or not to be, itself.'[2] Two procedures now become possible. The first is the one espoused by the *existentiel* thinkers, whose aim is to apprehend and clarify what this means,

[1] *Sein und Zeit*, 12f.
[2] *Ibid.*, 12.

so that the self, whether in oneself or in others, may attain thereby to true selfhood. The other is his own approach, the *existential* one. This is not ethical, as the other is. It raises and seeks to answer a theoretical question, that of the 'ontological structure' of *Existenz*. Heidegger wishes to analyse and set out what constitutes this; he approaches it as something to be studied, not as something to be won or lost.

That being the case, what justification is there for including Heidegger in the present study? One answer would be that his standpoint is not as purely theoretical as his language would suggest, since it is only to an active participation in life that man's self-transcendence is revealed; only so does he become aware that he is never merely what he is, but must always *do something* about what he is. Another answer would be that it is precisely what in Heidegger's book lends itself to *existentiel* interpretation that has in fact been influential. The description of human life in *Sein und Zeit* stands out from the rest of the work as comparatively lucid. Moreover, the author himself spent so much pains upon it that some readers have suspected that, in the course of this exposition, he had lost interest in the larger problem of Being and would not return to it. In that, of course, they were mistaken, but the second part of the book is still unwritten or at least unpublished and the post-war essays from Heidegger's pen hardly enable us to surmise what form its argument would take, were it ever written. But, whether rightly or wrongly, the book as it stands has been a powerful influence on Continental thought, and I am here concerned with it from this point of view. That is to say, in what follows, I shall seek to show what *Sein und Zeit* has contributed to existentialism rather than to summarize its argument.

(*b*)

I said earlier in this chapter that Heidegger approaches the problem of Being by way of human life[1] as a privileged instance thereof, a case in which it is true that 'knowledge and being are one'. The attempt to analyse this is a phenomenological one. That is to say, it seeks to penetrate beneath the ready-made view of the world and human life with which we work in daily life and in science and to attain direct insight into what is to be described. Heidegger regards the whole modern world-view as erroneous and as substituting a construction of our own for that encounter with Being which was possible in the ancient world and even in the Middle Ages. The fundamental difference between the modern world and previous periods, he would say, is not that we have another world-picture than they had, but that we have a world-picture while they had nothing of the kind. Our science has constructed this scheme, with which it then approaches experience, prepared to accept as real and actual only what fits into this picture. The supreme instance of this is in physics,

[1] The rendering 'human life' for *Dasein* has at least this to be said for it, that it is English. 'Existence' would be better, but this word must be reserved for the special technical meaning given to *Existenz*. I have been quite shameless in using 'existential' and its derivatives for Heidegger, even where he would prefer 'existentiel'.

The Challenge of Death

where only what is measurable is accepted as having reality.[1]

When we state that the first characteristic of human life is that it is *being-in-the-world*, we mean therefore something quite different from what a science that is dominated by the Cartesian metaphysics would have us believe. Man is not a subject surrounded by objects. I must begin my analysis, not with man, but with myself. The world in which I am is, as it were, the circle of my preoccupation, the range over which my interest and concern operate. The world I live in is *my* world, since the only possible centre within it is myself. Everything is arranged around me and related to me, that is, to my purposes and not merely to my knowledge. A moment ago, while I was absorbed in typing, the footsteps downstairs and the train approaching the nearby station were not within my world. Now, when I pause for a moment and let my attention roam freely, they are. My world, therefore, is not a fixed quantity; it changes its pattern and its content from moment to moment. But always I am in it.

Yet, what is meant by saying that I am 'in' the world? We are apt to suppose that this refers to some kind of spatial inclusion; I am in the world as a knife is in my pocket. But there is a more original sense of being 'in', and this is the one intended here. I am in the world in the first instance in the sense of being actively concerned with it. The world of daily life is my environment, the range of things that affect me somehow and require me to take up an attitude to them; the

[1] *Holzwege* (1950), 69ff.

world of natural science and metaphysics is a much later construction out of this. The Greeks did not speak of 'things' but of *pragmata*, implying that I have to do something (*praxis*) about them. We may call them 'utensils', instruments available for my employment. Man is a tool-using animal in the sense that everything in his world is some kind of tool for him. None of these utensils exists as a thing, that is, an object taken in isolation and then needing to be related somehow to other objects similarly isolated, but only in a twofold relation. On the one hand, it is at the disposal of someone for some purpose of his, it is relative to human life. On the other, it is linked up with other utensils, is part of a system of such, indeed, of several systems, it may be, so that the significance it has within one of these may be quite different from the significance it has in another.[1]

But I am aware also of other persons who are in the world. I am not only 'in', I am also 'with'. The existence of other selves is not something needing to be deduced from my own: awareness of other selves is as primary as self-awareness. I only attain to self-consciousness within a network of relations to others.

---

[1] So my primary spatial judgments are relative to myself and my present interests. How far away the apple is that is just beyond the small boy's reach! Put him on a chair and it is near at once. The use of spatial terms to symbolize personal relations makes this clear. One person is remote because his manner makes him unapproachable, another is near to me because, though he may be in Australia for the time being, he is in sympathy with me and can be relied on to respond to an appeal. It is in this sense also that God is near or far. Space as the undifferentiated continuum in which objects are placed out while we, as disinterested spectators, merely take note of their positions, is an abstraction.

The Challenge of Death

Being-in-the-world is therefore being-with-others. These others are there not as isolated individuals with whom some sort of connection has to be established: the threads that bind us together are already spun, they belong to our selfhood. Others are there from the out-set in relation to myself: I am concerned about them, I have to take account of them in all that I do, and they have to do as much for me. As preoccupation governs our life with things, so concern governs our life with persons.

But who are these persons with whom I have to do? Or rather, who am I? Heidegger's interest in the analysis of being-with is that it may enable him to answer this question.

Here, as in our account of the world and the things within it, our standpoint is that of daily life, as yet unsophisticated by scientific conclusions or metaphysical theories. Who am I, not as the soul-substance of the philosopher, but as John Smith today? The answer is that in actual fact I am not a self at all, for the relation in which I stand to others turns out to be one of dependence, a radical and inescapable dependence. We stand at one another's beck and call, we have no life of our own, but only a constant effort to be and to do what others require of us. Who then are these others? They are no better off than myself: I represent to them the tyranny that cramps their life, the will, not their own, to which they must surrender theirs. We are all slaves. Who then is the master? The situation is worse than has just been described. For it is not that I tyrannize over others and they over me, but something impersonal in us all holds us in bondage. No one has seen this power that rules us, no one can give him a name. He is the 'they', the French *On*, the German *Man*. That is the 'subject' of experience in daily life. None of us is a self, he is consumer or producer, employer or employee. We are standardized, reduced to an average. Everything is determined by what 'they' will think or say and so on. We do not pass moral judgments, 'they' do. As the conscript says after a month's service: 'I never thought of doing this, that or the other before I joined the army; but everybody does it.' One is reminded here of Kierkegaard's tirades against the mass, and against the press and public opinion as two of its most dangerous embodiments. This tyranny comes to a head in the totalitarian state, but it exists among us all the while in less overt and apparently harmless forms. Thus, there is a common-sense view of the world that everybody works with but for which no one is ultimately responsible; there is a philosophy embodied in our language and we take it for granted; there are the moral judgments we do not make but which are made for us by the prevalent climate of opinion, and so on. These anonymous powers are at once outside us and of our own making. But we make them by ceasing to be ourselves and surrendering our freedom. Selfhood is sundered by an abyss from this impersonal tyranny.[1]

In his analysis of what he terms the sheer banality of

---

[1] 'Each one is the other and no one is himself. The "they" who is the answer to the question after the "who" of daily life is the "nobody" to whom we are all delivered over *en masse.' Sein und Zeit*, 128.

daily life, Heidegger singles out three special features. The first is *talk*, the mere chatter that fills up time when there is nothing worth saying, the gossip that repeats what has been said elsewhere, and so on. The second is *curiosity*, the quest for the new and the sensational, for seeing what things look like without any genuine desire to get to know them. The third is *ambiguity*, the art of concealment and manœuvre, so that one gives nothing away, and comes out on the right side in the end, whatever happens. We watch one another and act a part, we play for safety, hostility lurks behind a show of friendliness. All these are so many manifestations of the fallen condition that lies behind them and comes to expression in them. It is not meant, when one speaks of man as 'fallen', that there was some primitive happy condition he has lost. It is equally far from the truth to suppose that what is thus described is a state of things from which we may expect to rise with the progress of civilization. To be fallen means to be a prey to the world and to the 'they'. It is less a state than a movement from state to state. We are attracted and tempted by the world, we fall victims to it and then invent specious arguments to prove that all is as it should be, till we become estranged from ourselves, entangled and lost. 'Human life falls out of itself and into itself, into the bottomless abyss and nothingness of the inauthentic and the commonplace.'[1] We live as it were always in flight from ourselves.

I do not doubt that in this description of man as fallen Heidegger is drawing on the Christian tradition.

[1] *Ibid.*, 178.

The Challenge of Death

He insists, to be sure, that he passes no moral judgment but merely analyses and describes. Nevertheless, one may well doubt whether he would have seen what he does had his sight not been sharpened by his early Christian training. Bultmann can use his account of man to cast light on the concept of the flesh in Paul[1] and Thielicke can appropriate it as a faithful picture of modern man, unredeemed.[2] Nor is this to give a theological twist to something of a quite different order. For is it not clear that for Heidegger's vision, as for the Christian one, man is the being who is not what he ought to be?

(c)

Our procedure so far has been analytic. We have set to work as those would do who describe a nation in its various aspects, its geographical background, its historical development, its form of government. Something, however, remains unexpressed in all this, what we may term the specific character, the genius of the people. It may be approached in these various ways, but the results thus reached must then be taken up into a total apprehension. So it is here.

At this point we return to the experience of dread to which appeal was made in *What is Metaphysics?* Dread is not fear. Fear is concerned with particular interests: I fear to lose my watch or my train or my reputation or my family. But dread is not for any object that can be named in this fashion: the threat it

[1] *Offenbarung und Heilsgeschehen* (1941), 49f.
[2] *Tod und Leben* (1947).

31

encounters is at once nowhere and everywhere, it is indefinite yet compelling. In the last resort, dread is for oneself and for what is involved in being-in-the-world. It corresponds to the fact that we are ill at ease in the world, not at home there. If it is urged that most people seem rather to be very much at ease in the world, Heidegger replies that this is only so much evasion. When we feel ourselves at home in the world, it is because we dare not face the grim fact of our homelessness and so resort to all kinds of expedients to conceal it from ourselves. We are fundamentally ill at ease here, estranged, we do not belong, however we may pretend that we do.

Dread is the psychological phenomenon that reveals to us what constitutes our life. This is care (*Sorge*). Dread is the point at which care breaks through and comes to light, forcing upon our attention what otherwise might have gone unnoticed. Here we have a dynamic view of life, which has nothing in common with the Cartesian view of the self as a substance. For care is not, as we might suppose, an activity in which the self engages. There is no permanent self that 'feels' care. Care is what I am. It is prior to the self, and this is not given to me, it has to be won. The permanence of the self is the steadfastness and continuity, the blending of past, present, and future that arise out of the resolution characteristic of authentic existence. At the level of commonplace life and its banalities there is as yet nothing to be dignified with the name of a self. I am restless, feverish care.

Three features of this care we are and do not merely

32

have may be briefly summarized. First, it is a concern for the self and its possibilities that is continually running on ahead. Man is the being who is for ever taking thought for the morrow, he is a series of projects flung forward into the future. His scientific, political, economic, even his religious activities are so many anticipations of the future and attempts to secure himself therein. A man only lives for the present, we may say, because he feels that his birthright is the future and this is for some reason denied to him. Second, care is occupied with a world that is simply given to it, not chosen by it. We were *thrown* here, we are conscripts and not volunteers in the army of the living. Life has its basis in brute fact. The awakening to consciousness is the discovery that we were here, so to speak, in advance of ourselves. Third, care is actively engaged with the utensils and tasks of the world in association with others. It is busy and anxious about many things. Thus, care contains within itself the three forms of temporality, future, past, and present in that order of significance.

Let me pause here to stress the importance of this priority of the future in the analysis of our experience of time. Of course, the time-scheme with which we work, the series of consecutive moments, each of which is exactly the same as the others because all are empty of content, like so many tiny boxes in which events are somehow inserted—this time-scheme is a later and artificial product of abstract thinking. Man is a being who looks forward before he looks back. He writes history in order that he may be more adequate to the urgent moment at which he must take down the tent of the present and go forth, a wanderer, into the future. Once this truth about man is grasped, no arguments for freedom are any longer needed: so to be constituted is what freedom means. Where the past has priority, on the other hand, determinism reigns.

It is to be noticed that the analysis and appreciation of human life in this and the previous section are not from any vantage-ground outside it. What we have been concerned with is self-knowledge, first in the form of mood, vague rapport or lack of rapport with oneself, and then with a more definite attempt to understand human life as that in which one is involved. The portrait of man that has been drawn is thus a self-portrait. But it shows him not as a thing to be studied, but as a ceaseless activity, an openness to the future. In other words, it shows him rather as a potentiality than as an actuality: what he is is finally what he has it in him to become. He sees himself always as one to whom he has to take up an attitude, about whom he has to do something. That is surely what is meant by saying that he is care. A being who lives with his face towards the future asks himself all the while: 'What am I to become?'

(*d*)

Unfortunately, the question has already received the wrong answer. Man, it would appear, has opted not to become himself, but to sink himself in the world and in the mass. The account of man that has been given thus far, of man as cluttered up with preoccupations,

34

The Challenge of Death

obsessed with what others think, and reduced to the average—this is not finally a description of what he is, but rather of what he has chosen to be. For self-knowledge is the privilege of man, and once he knows what he is he has to decide whether to continue as such or to become otherwise. The existence described is inauthentic existence, the condition of one who is other than he ought to be. But this clearly implies that, estranged though he is from himself, he is not wholly lost to himself. The possibility of authentic existence stands open to him. He is aware of this, not by any revelation from God, but in virtue of the self-illuminating power of human life as such; it carries within itself a capacity for understanding itself. But what is the perspective from which it can be seen that the existence we have spoken of is in fact inauthentic? The perspective is that of death, the one thing in human life we have hitherto left out of the picture.

Of course, we cannot leave it out. We cannot regard it as a strange accident that happens to life. It is rather an essential characteristic of life, as perhaps nothing else is. When you stand by the cradle of a new-born child, there is only one statement you can make of him with entire certainty. He will die. In daily life with its thoughtlessness we suppose that we can evade this fact. We do so by taking refuge in the assertion that death is the common lot; we make it our duty to keep from those about us the knowledge of their impending death. It is not a subject we care to talk about; because it may happen at any time, we persuade ourselves that it will always happen to other people and not to us.

The Challenge of Death

How many pilots who take off for a long-distance bombing raid seriously imagine that they will not come back? The right attitude to death is to envisage it as involved in life. Death is not the axe that cuts down the tree, it is the fruit that grows on it.

Death so understood isolates me and makes of me an individual. It is my death, not that of the multitude to which I belong. Each of us dies his own death. It forces me to detach myself from all that binds me to the world and to others, for I must separate myself from them in dying. It cannot be repeated: I can sit an examination twice, compare my second marriage with my first, and so on. I die only once. Death is the extreme threat, for it robs us not of this or that utensil, but of that whole condition of being-in-the-world without which we simply are not. It is so challenging because it is at once certain and uncertain: *that* it will come is certain, *when* it will do so is uncertain. It rounds off my life, yet I can never know how it does so, never look back on my life as a completed whole, for in the moment that ends it I am no more. There is nothing morbid about this steady contemplation of death; accusations of that kind are merely the device of the impersonal 'they' to prevent our escaping its tyranny and becoming individuals. What is necessary is to see our life as a being-towards-death.[1]

Once this point has been reached, there is a possibility of deliverance from the banality of everyday life

---

[1] See Lehmann: *Der Tod bei Heidegger und Jaspers* (1938), Wach: *Das Problem des Todes in der Philosophie unserer Zeit* (1934), Jolivet: *Le Problème de la Mort chez Heidegger et J.-P. Sartre* (1950).

and its servitude to anonymous powers. He who has so confronted his death is stabbed awake thereby. He perceives himself now as an individual distinct from the mass and is prepared to take over responsibility for his own life. There is a paragraph to this effect that defies translation, but I will offer a paraphrase:

'As we run ahead in thought towards death we become aware that we are lost in the impersonal, public self, and we are faced with the possibility of being ourselves. But to be ourselves we must refuse any support that others offer us in their concern about us and for us. We must abandon all illusions and, combining passionate intensity with acceptance of fact, enter upon freedom-to-death as something at once certain and fraught with dread.'[1]

In this way we decide for authentic against inauthentic existence. We emerge from the mass and become ourselves at last.[2]

This salvation of man from bondage is his own work, as the passage cited above makes quite clear. There is therefore something in man that protests against his lost condition and bears witness to another possibility. This is *conscience*, which calls each man out

[1] *Sein und Zeit*, 266. A literal rendering is given in *Existence and Being*, 78. There is surely an echo here of Kierkegaard's emphasis on despair as the prelude to salvation. Cf. Rilke on 'the great death, which each man carries within himself'.

[2] It is at this point that the closest connection is established between an *existentiel* and an *existential* attitude. For the former alone reveals those aspects of human life which the latter describes. *Ibid.*, 248f., 266. On the whole question of the non-moral attitude of Heidegger as opposed to Kierkegaard's see now Løgstrup: *Kierkegaards and Heideggers Existenzanalyse und ihr Verhältnis zur Verkündigung* (1950). For Heidegger's own judgment on Kierkegaard see *Holzwege*, 230. He 'is no thinker, but a religious writer'.

of the mass and speaks to him as an individual self. Its call comes to him in silence.

'It is never the case that the call is of our own planning, or is prepared for or brought about by willing on our part. The call comes, against our expectation and even against our will. On the other hand, the call certainly does not come from someone else who is in the world with me. It comes from me and yet over me.'[1]

Conscience is not a separate faculty in man: it is the voice of care, with which we are familiar already. It is that expression of care that ministers to authentic existence, while we were concerned previously with care as expressed in inauthentic existence. It makes us aware of guilt. By this is not meant being guilty of this or that specific fault, but being guilty of a radical defect in human life that makes such faults and therefore such guilt possible. This arises from the fact that, as has been said, we are thrown into the world, we are not here as volunteers but as conscripts. We are free, but we did not choose our freedom: we are called to account for what we are; yet we have no option in the matter. Also, we exist only in our projects, in the care that takes thought for the future and sketches out a possibliity on its as yet untouched canvas. But the realization of any one possibility carries with it the rejection of others, so that negation and exclusion are woven into the fabric of life. Here again we see how Being only is as it is haunted by Nothing.[2]

[1] *Ibid.*, 275.

[2] 'Freedom *is* only in the choice of some one possibility, therefore in acceptance of the fact that we have not chosen the others and cannot add the choice of them to our present choice.' *Ibid.*, 285.

The Challenge of Death

Through the realization of our guilt we pass to *resolution* as the act by which the self becomes a whole, free, and authentic. As such, we are not taken out of the world but given a new perspective on it, so that all relations to it now express our selfhood. Nor are we isolated from our fellows by the attainment of selfhood, but now for the first time we are capable of genuine fellowship with them, seeing and respecting in them something of the freedom we have ourselves won. He who has shaken off the tyranny of the mass looks on men with new eyes: they are henceforth persons for him, no longer nameless entities, partners in a common enterprise, no longer victims of the same conditions. To be sure, we must live in the same public world as before, handling its utensils, but as its masters and not as its slaves.

What happens may be described as the transmutation of circumstances into situations. Circumstances are events that happen to me and to which I stand in no inward relation. A situation, on the other hand, is an organization of possibilities, a realm of conditions that I take over from the world and my own past and in which I am called to exercise my freedom.

As we look back on this whole description of how authentic existence is reached and maintained, we are once more conscious of the Christian roots of Heidegger's thinking. However he may assure us that he does not mean by terms like conscience and guilt what the theologian means by them, it is doubtful whether he would have used such terms at all had they not been put at his disposal by the tradition in which he stands.

Yet, the final outcome is reminiscent rather of Buddh-
ism than of Christianity. The man he envisages as free
and authentic has some features of the Arahant. He is
his own saviour.

'Therefore, O Ananda, be ye lamps unto yourselves.
Be ye a refuge to yourselves. Betake yourselves to no
external refuge. Hold fast to the Truth as a lamp. Hold
fast as a refuge to the Truth. Look not for refuge to
any one beside yourselves.'[1]

(e)

Heidegger's thought is so complex and so searching
that it seems overbold to claim that one has understood
him. It is so easy to read him with the presuppositions
in one's mind that have governed European philosophy since Plato, when, as we shall see more definitely
in the next section, he is out to challenge and reject
those presuppositions.

In so far, however, as I have understood him, there
are four main criticisms I would offer, two concerned
with his thought as a whole and two with specific
points in it.

1. The first criticism might be introduced by asking
what judgment Kierkegaard would pass on *Sein und
Zeit* were he to return to life and read it. I suspect that
he would accuse it of evasion. It would seem to him
that Heidegger has found a new way to do what Hegel
did, to exploit basic Christian ideas for philosophy
while emasculating them in the process. Words that

[1] Rhys Davids: *Dialogues of the Buddha* (1910), Part II, 108.

originally had an ethical reference are employed by him in what he insists is a non-ethical connection. He diagnoses man's condition as fallen and describes how the sense of guilt leads on to salvation, but God himself does not enter the process at any point. More serious is the fact that he claims to be observing and describing where he should be deciding. If the human predicament is as he describes it, then—so Kierkegaard would say—one has no right to spend time over analysing its structure, one should do something about it. This kind of existentialism is simply not existentialist enough. If one were to reply to Kierkegaard that after all a philosopher's calling is to analyse and describe, conversion is not for his pages but for his life, he might well defend himself by naming others who have written philosophy so that it vibrates with spiritual passion for the reader, and becomes what Jaspers speaks of as freedom calling to freedom. Heidegger has carried too far the secularization of Christian dogma: if there is as much truth in this as his borrowings imply, he ought to have taken it more seriously.

2. His description of human life is vitiated by a fault of method. What he has actually done is to isolate certain aspects of human life and then to pass off the resulting account as though it were a faithful picture of the whole. The inauthentic existence of which he speaks is an abstraction, he would have us take it as the reality. He has proved his thesis by first emptying daily life of all the meaning it contains, so leaving it dull, banal, and enslaved, and then importing meaning into it by a heroic decision. In this he has acted just as the

41

theologians do who remove everything of God from human life and history, in order to be able to introduce these subsequently as grace and revelation entirely from the Beyond. In each case, the result is reached by shutting one's eyes to all that would challenge the prejudice with which one approaches the evidence. For example, Heidegger has in view not man as such, but man in urban society as we know it today in the West, surrounded by a mechanized environment. Nature does not seem to enter the picture at any point. I doubt whether a hiker, roaming on a summer day through the Lake District, really thinks of his environment as a complex of interrelated tools. Or, for that matter, whether a Chinese gentleman of the old style did. No notice is taken of the hundred and one graces that adorn daily life for most of us, the unexpected kindlinesses we receive, and—for those who have eyes to see it—the presence of God in it all. We have been given a caricature of daily life instead of a portrait.

3. I doubt, too, whether the passage from inauthentic to authentic existence is normally due in this way to death. As we shall find, this is one of the points at which Sartre does not follow Heidegger. It is no doubt the case that death for man is something much more than the break-up of the biological organism. Man can anticipate his death as the animal cannot, he can run forward to it in thought and so make a problem of it. Man dies as guilty, as one who has neglected opportunities, as one who injured others and can no longer hope to repair the wrong he did them. Death would be no problem were man without a conscience. 'The sting

of death is sin; and the power of sin is the law.' Still, when one stands in imagination by the mass-grave in which thousands of victims, whether of aerial bombardment or totalitarian cruelty, have been buried, one wonders whether death has in fact the individualizing potency the argument assigns to it. True, Heidegger might reply that, though it does not have this effect, it *ought* to have it, and this is all he is concerned to maintain. But are we not actually awakened to selfhood more often in other and worthier ways, by giving and receiving love, by a lofty example, by inescapable responsibilities, or even by wise guidance that insists from our earliest years on our learning to be persons?

4. This over-emphasis on death is accompanied by a striking indifference to birth. And yet may not the import of life reveal itself more adequately in its *terminus a quo* than in its *terminus ad quem?* True as it is that we are 'thrown' into the world, that we did not ask to be sent here, that is only part of the truth. Does it mean nothing that birth is connected with an act that, however biological at one level, is at another spiritual, involves indeed the whole personalities of those who engage in it as the mutual dedication of one man and one woman? Does not this suggest that a new life enters the world as a gift from the older lives, a dower they contribute out of the riches they have themselves received? Life is intimately bound up with love. In view of this, is it possible to dismiss without consideration the Christian view of life as a trust from God? There seems to be nothing in the world as Heidegger sees it that can be termed sacred: yet is not

human life shot through with this quality? Human life is related not only to the world and not only to other instances of human life; it has an ultimate reference that manifests itself in these references of a lower order. A commonplace action such as the purchase of the week's rations is not necessarily nor always a routine one merely. It provides an opportunity for the meeting of person with person, for moral choices and therefore for responsibility for the other before God. The truth about man is only known when he is seen in the presence of God.

But are we justified in accusing Heidegger of relativism and atheism? To this we now turn.

(f)

Two of Heidegger's post-war publications deal with the problem of truth[1] and they enable us to do more justice than we might otherwise have done to the discussion of this subject in *Sein und Zeit*. There he used language that certainly gave many readers the impression that for him all meaning in the world is of human origin, that man as it were imposes significance on what originally possessed none. All truth, it was affirmed, is relative to man. 'The Newtonian laws, the principle of contradiction, any and every truth, are true only so long as human reality is.'[2] It is not meant, of course, that certain laws were false before Newton discovered them, but that they were not laws at all,

[1] *On the Essence of Truth*, translated in *Existence and Being*, 317ff.
[2] *Sein und Zeit*, 226.

44

since a law is only such as it is known. The human mind knows what is; take away the human mind and what is does not vanish, it just is not known. When we assert that the world would remain as it is now for us were there no one there to know it, we are really imagining what the world would be like were *we* to know it with no one else there! We have only to reflect what we mean when we speak of a natural catastrophe as 'senseless'. It has no meaning because it has none for us. Once we can relate it in some way to ourselves, we incorporate it into the realm of the significant.[1] So that to raise the question—as the metaphysician does—of the meaning of Being, is not to imply that there is something behind Being that invests it with significance. We are asking what Being is in so far as it becomes intelligible to us.

This position is not to be confused with that of Kant, for whom man as the subject of knowledge orders and gives meaning to the raw material made available through the senses. 'The understanding gives laws to nature.' For Heidegger, man is much more than the subject of knowledge; truth and error are his, not in virtue of his understanding, but as a total self. Let us seek to outline how this is.

There is a time-honoured definition of truth as *adaequatio rei et intellectus*. We have a representation or we form a judgment: this is true when it corresponds to the reality, erroneous when it does not. Yes, but how do we have access to the reality so as to be able to effect the comparison? The traditional concept of truth

[1] *Ibid.*, 152.

rests on another concept that needs to be made explicit. For the Greeks, truth was *aletheia*, a privative formed from *lanthano*, I conceal. There is truth only when Being discloses itself, draws the veil. It is the peculiar privilege of man that this disclosure is made to him. We may say that he is characterized by openness to Being, capable of receiving its revelation. Or we may say that whereas everything else is in the world, he stands out from it, he *ek-sists*. He thus occupies a point of vantage from which two perspectives are possible. One is upon Being itself: it shines by its own light, but it shines upon man, he alone can as it were catch its rays. But he can also observe and concentrate his attention upon particular objects around him, in which case his vision of Being becomes blurred. Man, to put the same thing in another way, has the capacity to let things be, to accept them simply as they are. This indeed is what constitutes his freedom: other things are merely played upon passively, man is active even in the influences he receives from beyond himself.[1] This openness, this letting things be, this freedom are the source at once of our human advance and of our great loss. For knowledge tends to the particular, it singles out the part for attention and study, and so loses the vision of the whole. We are hypnotized by the intelligible and the practicable, and the mystery that pervades our being fades into the light—and an artificial light at that!—of common day. This is the source of all our error. What we have here is a restatement, in as difficult

---

[1] But not active in the Kantian sense: man is free when he allows Being to have its full rights over him, not when he employs it for his own purposes.

and obscure a language as philosophy can invent, of the old truth that 'knowledge grows, but wisdom lingers'. In this sense, Heidegger would have us return from our specialization and technical achievements to the vision of pure Being and so begin again.

Heidegger is concerned primarily with this process of error and deterioration as reflected in the history of Western philosophy. Sometimes the guilty party is Plato, who interposed the concept between man and Being with his theory of Ideas.[1] Sometimes again it is Descartes, who reduced the concrete individual to a mere instance of the impersonal subject and gave him a world of dead things to know and manipulate.[2] These two examples enable us to build a bridge linking up the post-war lectures and essays with *Sein und Zeit*. Inauthentic existence is correlated with error, authentic existence with truth. By the one we are lost in a world of utensils and merged in the mass, because we have imposed a pattern of our own upon what we should have been content to let be. When we take the latter course, we establish that mysterious connection with Being which enables us to enter into possession of our selves. Truth is thus rather a quality of personal life than a property of our judgments. We are reminded of the Fourth Gospel, where the truth is not only known, but also done.[3]

We can now understand in what sense Heidegger is anti-humanist. He is opposed to any doctrine of man

[1] *Platons Lehre von der Wahrheit* (1947).
[2] *Holzwege*, 80 ff.
[3] 'He that doeth the truth cometh to the light, that his works may be made manifest, that they are wrought in God.' John, iii, 21.

47

as such, because this necessarily involves his reduction to the average, makes him an object and in so doing robs him of his freedom. It is one more way in which we impose ourselves on what we should let be. Similarly, he denies values in the sense that values for him are man-made, nets with which we catch what is, in order that we may choose and reject according to some convenience of our own. If he is anti-humanist in this sense, it is because he seeks something higher than either humanism or its repudiation. He is no spokesman for barbarism, since barbarism in its turn is another man-made pattern.

The repudiation of subjectivity in the later works goes beyond what might have been expected by the reader of *Sein und Zeit*. There the impression left on us is that of the lonely, heroic, strong man who takes his destiny into his own hands: the call of conscience is from himself and not from beyond himself. Yet, in the light of the later development of Heidegger's thought, it would seem better to say that he listens to the call of Being, and that surely is from beyond the human, as he now seems to say. The difference is somewhat reduced if we identify the consciousness of death with the awakening to the mystery of Being, as perhaps we should. Death is the point at which knowledge fails and we become open to Being. While the gap may be narrowed in this way, I think that it still remains to some extent.

A few words only are necessary on Heidegger's atheism. Here, also, as shown in his analysis of what Nietzsche may be taken to mean by his slogan: 'God is

The Challenge of Death

dead', it is the God men have constructed for themselves, whether as the Supreme Being or the Supreme Value, he rejects. This is the God whom we have murdered; that is, the metaphysical thinking of the West filed its petition in bankruptcy with Nietzsche. We have reached the point at which not only do our categories break down, but thinking in categories must be abandoned for the encounter with Being in its naked majesty.[1] Perhaps in the end, as the Nothing is necessary to Being, as death awakens us to life, as the repudiation of the science of man opens the way to man himself, whom no science can measure, so Nietzsche's so-called nihilism may be the quest for an affirmation that will give certainty, and the repudiation of the God we have known may be the first step on the way to the true God for whom he yearns.

The point at which we seem to arrive is mysticism, the *via negativa* of the scholastics, the Buddhist Nirvana as ineffable bliss. The ultimate reality is beyond all our reasoning and our language breaks down in any attempt to describe it. The only language that is not altogether inadequate for this purpose would seem to be that of the poet, especially Hölderlin.[2] But he would indeed be a bold man who should attempt to follow Heidegger when he enters this territory.

[1] *Holzwege*, 193ff.
[2] *Existence and Being*, 291ff. 'Hölderlin and the Essence of Poetry.'

3. Man and his Freedom[1]

I HAVE already said that Sartre follows Heidegger in the application of Husserl's phenomenological method to the problem of Being. We might indeed state the relation between the three men in the form of a Hegelian triad. Husserl's interest was in consciousness, and his main bequest to posterity was a phenomenological psychology. Heidegger, on the other hand, bypassed consciousness: throughout *Sein und Zeit* he shows himself interested in what consciousness discloses and not at all in what does the disclosing. What Sartre offers is a 'total phenomenology'. He is concerned with man-in-situation, with consciousness and its object in indissoluble relation.[2] As Husserl affirmed, intentionality is the fundamental characteristic of consciousness. That is to say, there can be no consciousness that is not directed upon an object. Neither, adds Sartre, can there be an object apart from a consciousness for which it is object. There is no dualism in this. We do not deal first with one and

---

[1] I am greatly indebted throughout this chapter to Jeanson: *Le Problème moral et la Pensée de Sartre* (1947). What makes this book of special importance is the preface by Sartre himself, in which he endorses the interpretation of his thought given in it.

[2] Jeanson: *Op. cit.*, 138f.

then with the other, but with them both in the relation
binding them together. Of course, for the purpose of
study it is necessary to separate them. This yields at the
outset the distinction between two types of being.
With this we enter upon Sartre's distinctive contribution to ontology, in the distinction he seeks to establish
between the *in-itself* and the *for-itself*.

(*a*)

Sartre is opposed to any attempt to eliminate either
the subject or object by absorbing it in the other. His
phenomenology is not phenomenalism, it knows nothing either of a mysterious thing-in-itself that lurks
inaccessible behind phenomena or of the self of idealism that produces its own content; nor does he reduce
consciousness to a mere epiphenomenon. Each retains
for him its own full rights.

The *in-itself* is simply there, solid, massive, and un-
questionable. We perceive it, but that does not mean
that its *esse* is *percipi*. We perceive it as that which is
independent of ourselves. It is neither active nor passive, neither affirmative nor negative; it is beyond all
our categories, for it simply *is*. It does not exist for
itself, since it is identical with itself. Indeed, all such
language is sadly misleading, for it introduces a divi-
sion into the *in-itself*, whereas this is in a region where
relation to itself does not arise. It lies beyond becoming, it cannot be opposed to anything else. We
may not say that it is possible or that it is necessary.
There is just one term, perhaps, that we can apply

to that before which all terms break down. We can say of it that it is contingent, merely accidental, just there.

What then of the *for-itself* or consciousness? As was said above, consciousness apprehends the object as other than itself: whatever it is, it is aware of itself as not that. In the most elementary dealing with the object, therefore, it must go beyond itself, transcend itself, as Sartre would say. But consciousness is not merely a mirror held up to the object to reflect it; it can take stock of it, ask questions about it. Let us contemplate for a moment this intriguing phenomenon of interrogation. For a question admits of two answers, one affirmative and the other negative, and it considers these as equally possible. So that for the questioner what *is not* is a possibility alongside of what is. If the first formula for being runs 'Being is', the second runs 'Being is *that*, and outside that, *nothing*.'[1] We are back again at the problem that haunted Heidegger. 'That we are able to say no, requires as its necessary condition, that non-being should be a perpetual presence, within us and beyond us.'[2]

The Nothing cannot belong to Being, yet it cannot be apart from it. The solidity of Being that we were admiring so recently has suffered injury. It is as if it had been torn. A hole has appeared in it. The only possible source of this catastrophe—we are using admittedly mythical terms—is consciousness. For consciousness not merely is, it distinguishes itself from the *in-itself*,

---

[1] *L'Être et le Néant*, 40.
[2] *Ibid.*, 46f.

it is the creator of distinctions and categories, in virtue
of which we have to reckon not only with what a thing
is but also with what a thing is not. For consciousness,
indeed, the two approaches are inseparable. Try describing something and before long you will find yourself contrasting it with something else and saying that
it is not that. Consciousness possesses the power to
form that mysterious sentence we have just quoted:
Being is *that*, and outside that, *nothing*.

But whence does consciousness derive this power to
infect Being with Nothing? This is only possible because consciousness somehow secretes the Nothing
within itself. 'Man is the being by whom the Nothing
comes into the world.'[1] Consciousness is not this or
that object, it is not any object at all. But surely it is
itself? No, that is precisely what it is not. Consciousness
is never identical with itself. Thus, when I reflect upon
myself, the self that is reflected is other than the self
that reflects. When I try to state what I am, I fail because while I am speaking, what I am talking about
slips away into the past and becomes what I was. I am
my past and my future; and yet I am not; I have been
the one and I shall be the other. It is never possible for
me to say to the self fleeting past me, 'Tarry, that I may
possess you!' So we may say that 'the being by whom
the Nothing arrives in the world is a being for whom,
in his being, it is a question of the Nothingness of his
being.'[2] Or that *consciousness is, not as what it is, but as
what it is not and what it is to be.*

[1] *Ibid.*, 60.
[2] *Ibid.*, 59.

Man and his Freedom

Consciousness is not therefore like a thing, solid, complete, full and given. It is process and self-creation, continual improvisation based on the rejection of what it has been up to this moment. To be is to spurn from one what one has been: in so far as one does not do that, one approximates to a thing and ceases to be a person. Man has the characteristic of self-transcendence, he lives by his projects, his sketches of possible courses of actions in the future. Man is for ever sending his thoughts on ahead of himself; he is as something to be surpassed, if we may apply to the individual what Nietzsche said of the race. In plain language, man is free. Or rather, man is freedom. You may say that freedom is the essence of man or that in man existence precedes essence. 'Man first *is*—only afterwards is he this or that . . . man must create for himself his own essence.'[1] As Sartre has told us more than once, he is here repudiating the Christian doctrine of creation in the Platonized form it assumed in the Middle Ages. It was supposed that God had certain ideas present to his mind as the patterns after which he created objects, man included. Each man therefore brings into the world something we call human nature, of which he is a particular instance. So his individuality can never be more than the realization of something that was originally included within his essence or nature. When this religious conception was secularized in the eighteenth century, it was still thought that there is a human nature common to all men. For Sartre, however, there is no God and therefore no human nature; man brings

[1] Quoted in Foulquié: *Existentialism* (1948), 64.

himself into being, not as an object in space and time, but as an activity of freedom, and what corresponds to essence or nature can only be a certain uniformity of structure that is afterwards discovered within the various instances of human freedom.[1]

(b)

Never before, unless perhaps in Schelling, has philosophy placed such an emphasis on freedom. Everything that follows will only serve to bring this out yet more clearly. But we must not expect from Sartre any lyrical praise of freedom as man's godlike privilege. True, it is literally godlike. That is to say, he has transferred to man the freedom Christianity—at least as Descartes understood it—ascribes to God. Descartes had an intuition of his own liberty, but could only explicate this in the language of his time and within the framework of Christain dogma. Hence he makes man free only to err, to refuse consent where ideas are not convincingly and irresistibly clear. God, however, is absolutely free and creative, so that the Good and the True exist solely by his will. Here we have what human liberty really is, since Descartes grants that it is one and the same in man and God. He had not the courage to draw this conclusion. Sartre has

[1] Foulquié, in my judgment, has missed the point when he distinguishes between the universal essence that is given to us and the individual essence we realize in freedom (*Ibid.*, 64). These both belong to the structure that comes to light within the exercise of freedom, so they both follow on existence logically. In the same way, my character is the consistency my free activity carries within itself.

done so, and he makes man the creator of values as though he were absolute freedom like God.

For Sartre, there is no God and man has all the freedom there is. But no one has given it to him, he just finds that he has it. There is no sense in saying that we *ought* to be free, for we just cannot be otherwise. If I sell myself as slave or surrender my will to a dictator, I exercise my freedom in so doing. The evasion of freedom is possible only by a free act. I could end my freedom by suicide, but how can man assert his freedom more intensely than by suicide? In this act, he disposes of himself in unrestricted sovereignty. We are 'condemned to be free'.[1] There we reach the limit of our freedom. I choose whatever I do, indeed whatever I am: but I did not choose to be free. I was forced into that. Of course, all such language is mythical, a survival from the days when men believed that a power beyond the human had given them life and set them in the world.

Man in his freedom is creative, indeed, he is the only creativity there is. The world outside him, the dull, solid world of the *in-itself* possesses neither significance nor value. He must confer these upon it or they will not be. It is by man that the distinction between good and evil emerges, therefore the distinction is always a human and a relative one. We do not merely choose between this course of action and that, we choose and make ourselves. And we must first choose the pattern, the standards according to which we make ourselves. Even if, in what Sartre calls the spirit of

[1] *Existentialism and Humanism* (1948), 34.

seriousness, we take over standards ready-made from tradition or other people or God, we can only do so by a free decision. And these standards would possess no value for us apart from our recognition. Values are fashioned by us out of our sense of need and our projects for the satisfaction of those needs. 'We have neither behind us, nor before us in a luminous realm of values, any means of justification or excuse. We are left alone, without excuse.'[1]

This is indeed 'dreadful freedom', as it has been called.[2] As such, it cannot but evoke anguish.

'I emerge alone and in anguish in face of the unique and primary project that constitutes my being. All barriers and railings collapse, annihilated by the consciousness of my liberty. I neither have nor can have any value in which to take refuge from the fact that it is I who maintain values in being. Nothing can guarantee me against myself. Cut off from the world and my essence by this nothing that I *am*, I have to realize the meaning of the world and of my essence. I decide it, alone, unjustifiable, and without excuse.'[3]

Suppose, however, one withdraws from freedom and observes it as something that simply is, what then? Then it seems to sink into an in-itself, to change from what I am to something I merely have. As such it is unjustifiable and absurd, absurd in the technical sense

[1] *Ibid.*, 34.

[2] Marjorie Grene: *Dreadful Freedom* (1948).

[3] *L'Être et le Néant*, 77. 'This nothing that I *am*', because my liberty consists in continual detachment from what I have been: I am free in so far as I am not exhausted by what I am but can become something more and something new. On this anguish before freedom, see also the passage quoted in Foulquié: *Existentialism*, 72.

that it lies in a region beyond all justification. It is sheer contingency, as stupid as the slight deviation in the flight of the Lucretian atoms, making it possible for them to cohere and for a world to arise.[1] It evokes now, not dread, but disgust, nausea. In *The Diary of Antoine Roquentin*, we have a vivid description of just such an emotional state.

'I dreamed vaguely of killing myself to wipe out at least one of these superfluous lives. But even my death would have been *In the way*. *In the way*, my corpse, my blood on these stones, between these plants, at the back of this smiling garden. And the decomposed flesh would have been *In the way* in the earth which would receive my bones, at last, cleaned, stripped, pealed, proper and clean as teeth, it would have been *In the way:* I was *In the way* for eternity.'[2]

So freedom appears from outside, that is, to inauthentic existence. It is seriously to misunderstand Sartre to suppose that he is describing a condition with which he is satisfied. He is not. He writes thus to shock his reader out of such a condition by showing him just what it is like.

(c)

We have been concerned so far with freedom in general. We now go on to consider it from three points of view, first, in the individual as a centre of freedom, next, in the relation between individuals, and finally, in

[1] Simone de Beauvoir: *Pour une Morale de l'Ambiguité* (1947), 36.
[2] *Op. cit.* (1949), 173.

Man and his Freedom

relation to the concrete situation within which freedom is exercised, within which alone it is in fact found.

The individual is a particular consciousness, that is, a particular irruption of freedom into the world. He is not cut out in advance into a particular pattern, but he carries his pattern within his activity. I am one unfolding of freedom, you another. We distinguish ourselves from the world as it is for each one of us; each of us is indeed the centre of reference and meaning for his world. Dead without us, it comes to life with and for us. My freedom is a constant unveiling of Being.[1] Our uniqueness consists in the fact that each of us does this in his own way.

Even more important is the fact that each of us enters into the future in his own way. For Sartre, as for Heidegger, man is the being who moves on ahead of himself. He anticipates the future, envisages its open possibilities as his own potentialities and takes up an attitude towards them. He is in and by the projects he forms, as I am at this moment as one who is forming the rest of this sentence in his mind and who looks forward beyond that to the completed book and its readers. Our projects are these outlines of contemplated action with which we go forward. It is the nature of freedom thus to look ahead. What it is not as yet but aims at being we call value; this is what a particular freedom sees to be desirable for itself, it lacks it and seeks it. It imagines that the attainment of the value in

[1] For a striking picture of what this means see the passage quoted from Simone de Beauvoir's novel in Foulquié: *Existentialism*, 76f. 'She was the only being to release the meaning of these abandoned places, of these sleeping objects; she was there, and they belonged to her.'

question would bring satisfaction: having reached its goal, freedom could then rest. But that is impossible in the nature of the case. For to be satisfied would be to pass into the condition of a thing and to cease to be this ever-advancing, improvising freedom. Freedom can only live and grow at the price of constant frustration. It is like Sisyphus rolling his stone up the hill and never able to reach the top. Man simply cannot cease to be free, however many attempts he makes to be rid of his freedom. Because the end he has in view always recedes, he fails. 'Man is a useless passion.'[1] This is not to be taken literally, of course. What is really meant is that valuation arises out of freedom and is inapplicable to it. Man is useless in the sense that it is from his decision that the terms 'useful' and 'useless' arise and it is only in relation to him that they have meaning.

Of course, man does not accept this condition as final; he spends his life in an attempt to achieve the impossible. He wants both to eat his cake and to have it, to unite being and existence, the solidity of the thing and the originality of the person. That is an aspiration to be God. For God is the only being in whom essence and existence are one, who combines absolute freedom with absolute necessity. He is the *ens realissimum* and the will that decides, with none to say it nay, what is good and evil. That is to say, men have thought of God in this way, but since the whole notion is inconsistent with itself, God cannot be. There can be no unity of the *in-itself* and the *for-itself*. There can be no being in whom essence and existence are one,

[1] *L'Être et le Néant*, 708.

since in the very nature of the case existence is contingent and therefore wholly other than essence.

It is the task of existential psycho-analysis to unveil this deception each man practises on himself by the effort to achieve the impossible. Sartre's *Baudelaire* is an application of the method.

'His dearest wish was to *be* like the stone and the statue enjoying the peaceful repose which belonged to the unchangeable; but he wanted this calm impenetrability, this total adhesion of the self to the self to be conferred on his free consciousness in so far as it was free and was consciousness.'[1]

It is important to see where this type of analysis differs from the Freudian. The latter is, in Sartre's eyes, one of the most reprehensible forms taken by the all-too-human desire to escape from freedom and the responsibility that accompanies it. If we accept the Freudian picture of the self, it is easy to think of ourselves as victims of circumstances beyond our control. We throw off guilt and responsibility on to a complex, a phobia, something that is not ourselves. We are cowardly or lustful, not because of anything we have done, but because someone treated us harshly or unwisely when we were infants. Or we think of ourselves as subtly deceived by the unconscious and the censor within. Sartre insists that there is no such mechanism within the self, that what appear as complexes, etc., are so many choices on our part. We are not divided into an unconscious that writes the script of a drama and a consciousness that perforce acts it, without under-

[1] *Op. cit.* (1949), 163f.

standing the lines it repeats. We are whole selves and our life is as we choose it to be. 'The existentialist says that the coward makes himself cowardly, the hero makes himself heroic; and that there is always a possibility for the coward to give up cowardice and for the hero to stop being a hero.'[1]

So it can be said of Baudelaire that 'every event was a reflection of that indecomposable totality which he was from the first to the last day of his life'. And again: 'We should look in vain for a single circumstance for which he was not fully and consciously responsible.'[2]

(d)

So much for the individual as a pattern of freedom. But I am also in the world along with other individuals. Their existence does not have to be deduced from mine, it is given along with mine. It is given above all in the experience of being observed, looked at. I am sitting in a public park on a summer day, enjoying the soft air, the sunshine, and the flowers. The whole scene is mine, it is organized around me and gives me pleasure. I notice a man on another seat reading a book, and I include him among the objects in my environment: for the moment, he is of less interest than the flower-

---

[1] *Existentialism and Humanism*, 43.

[2] *Op. cit.*, 185. Lest the reader should think that the existentialist shuts his eyes to the facts Freud has revealed as to the influence on our subsequent development of the earliest years, I may refer him to Simone de Beauvoir: *Pour une Morale de l'Ambiguité*, 51ff., where she shows how the wrong choices men make in later years are rooted in the infant's attitude to life. But they are always free decisions as to how that original attitude is to be continued or revised, never mere effects of it as a determining cause.

bed in front of me. Then, suddenly, he raises his head and looks at me. At once my valuation of him changes. I am aware of him no longer as one among many objects, but as something quite different, a subject. And, at the same time, my self-consciousness undergoes a change: I am aware of myself as object for him. Does he notice that I have an old suit on? Is he taking mental stock of me? If so, what does he think? I shall never know the answers to these questions, since he is a centre of freedom not open to invasion by me.

In such a situation, the other person is a menace. He introduces a disturbing factor into my world, which now is appropriated by someone else, who is in competition with me. My world has become his world, organized around him, with myself as merely one item in it. I am robbed of my dignity by the other. Even more devastating is what happens when one is listening through a key-hole and hears a step behind one. At such a time a person sees himself through the eyes of another and his whole conduct changes character accordingly. He becomes ashamed, and shame, as the story in Genesis iii suggests, accompanies the state of nakedness, of being exposed to someone else's gaze and judgment.

The other person is therefore my rival, simply by being other than myself. Once I have met him, he accompanies me inescapably. His picture of me, as I reconstruct it, has presented itself to my mind, and I have to do something about it. One possible reaction to it is surrender. I accept the other's picture of me as what I am and conform to it. In cowardice I lapse thereby from freedom to thinghood and am determined by another when I should be living out of myself. This, of course, is what we continually do. In the position we occupy, certain things are expected of us and we comply with those expectations. The doctor and the clergyman may lose the person in the official; the artist who leads a Bohemian life may do so because he knows that people are looking for him to do so; the politician says what his audience is waiting to hear him say. This is inauthentic existence with a vengeance.

What we call social life tends to promote play-acting rather than genuine communication, the intercourse of self with self. We may indeed imagine that we are leading others when in reality we are being determined by them: our success and popularity come to us solely because we assume the role they want us to assume. In one of his short stories Sartre has described a person who has thus taken himself over from others.

'The real Lucien—he knew now—had to be sought in the eyes of others, in the frightened obedience of Pierette and Guigard, the hopeful waiting of all those beings who grew and ripened for him, those young apprentices who would become his workers, the people of Ferolles, great and small, of whom he would one day be the master.'[1]

The story in question bears the title 'The Portrait of a Leader', and the passage cited brings out well how one who imagines he is dominating others is in fact the product of those others, made by their opinions and expectations.

[1] *Intimacy* (1949), 232.

Man and his Freedom

When we resolve to defend ourselves against the menace of the other, we do so by opening a counter-offensive. If he attempts to rob us of our liberty and reduce us to a mere thing, why should we not defeat him by doing that first to him? This is the struggle Hegel has analysed as one in which two consciousnesses 'prove themselves and each other through a life-and-death struggle'.[1] Any weapon is legitimate in the struggle in which we feel that our whole status as persons is in question. Is there no possibility of solidarity replacing conflict? Yes, there is, with the emergence of a third person. When two of us are under the observation of a third, we may make common cause against him. That is the origin of class-consciousness. The proletariat is made into a body with a common purpose because they have in the bourgeoisie a common antagonist. So Freud averred that the best way in which to unite people is to give them a common object of hatred. That indeed, as Bergson has shown, is the basis of the closed society: all Englishmen draw together against France, all Frenchmen against England—or Germany, as the case may be.

Where relations are closer and more personal, the conflict that results, and the complications introduced by the presence of a third party, form the theme of the play *In Camera*. The *dramatis personae* are introduced as dead, though they are not at first aware of this. Each presents himself to the others in a role he assumes so as to secure their approbation. But each sees that his own

[1] *Phenomenology of Mind* (1910), I, 179. The whole section on the master-slave relationship has influenced Sartre at this point.

65

prestige will be enhanced as he can expose the deceptions employed by the others. Pitiless conflict ensues, with shifting alliances of any two against the third, till the grim conclusion is drawn: 'Hell is . . . other people!'

All such attempts to defend ourselves against our rivals thus break down sooner or later. They end, as do all human actions, in frustration. But there is still one means open to us that promises better success. This is love. For in love I endeavour to disarm and appropriate the other, not by reducing him to an object, but by winning his consent to be mine. I lay siege to his freedom, I would secure myself against this by bringing about a situation in which he freely wills to be an ally and not a rival. Hence I am not satisfied with a single declaration that he is mine, I want this repeated, on oath if need be. I want to be sure that he will be mine always, to have him bind himself so that he can never again be free as against me. But clearly this effort also is doomed to frustration. For the moment I have persuaded the other to bind himself, I am secure against him indeed, but only by robbing him of his liberty. If, on the other hand, I preserve his liberty by not asking him to bind himself but leaving him free, where is my security? Yet it was for security that I entered upon the relation in the first instance. Love is the effort to appropriate another in his liberty, but liberty is something that, in the nature of the case, cannot be appropriated.

We need not follow Sartre in his description and analysis of other forms taken by the self to maintain its freedom over against the threat inherent in the freedom of another. I will only emphasize here, as already in a similar connection, that we must not suppose that Sartre is satisfied with relationships of this kind or that he regards them as the only ones possible. What he does maintain is that they are actual, that this is how in fact we live with one another, though we like to pretend otherwise. I shall have occasion to criticize him later on this head. At this stage, it is perhaps advisable to point out that much of what Sartre observes in human life had already been found there by Pascal.

'Human life is thus only a perpetual illusion; men deceive and flatter each other. No one speaks of us in our presence as he does in our absence. Human society is founded on mutual deceit; few friendships would endure if each knew what his friend said of him in his absence, although he then spoke in sincerity and without passion. Man is then only disguise, falsehood, and hypocrisy, both in himself and in regard to others. He does not wish anyone to tell him the truth; he avoids telling it to others, and all these dispositions, so removed from justice and reason, have a natural root in his heart.'[1]

We accept so severe a judgment from Pascal, because we know he has a remedy to propose. But so has Sartre, albeit a very different one.

(e)

We have still to deal with the obvious fact that our freedom is exercised only in certain limited and definite

[1] Pascal's *Pensées* (Everyman edition), 32f.

situations, I am, that is, I am as an Englishman of a certain age, physique, and social position, married, with two children, etc. I belong in the twentieth century with its fears of a third world war and its economic embarrassments and so on. This does not mean that my freedom is circumscribed by these conditions. My power is, but my freedom is not, and these are two distinct concepts. Freedom is not something that exists first of all in the air as it were and is somehow subsequently introduced into situations. My freedom only *is* within my situation: it is the use I make, from moment to moment, of my situation. It is ridiculous to say, for example, that the working-man is not free to start a daily newspaper: it is not in his power to do so. Freedom only exists within the area of those things that are within our power.

We might even say that my freedom is absolute just by being so relative in this sense. If I am a blind man, my freedom is absolute because what I do with my blindness is absolutely at my disposal: I decide it, sovereign and unfettered. It is true that my situation was not made by me, I was born to it or I came to it by someone else's act. Still, I make it mine by the very fact of consenting to live within it. Let us suppose that I was blinded by an explosion in a chemical factory. Then, while I did not choose to *become* blind, I choose to *be* such. I take over my blindness, make it my own act and an expression of my freedom by living with it. If you say that I had no alternative, I reply that I had. Others under like circumstances have committed suicide, so refusing blindness by an act of freedom. I considered that possibility and decided not to take it. The world is therefore justified in treating me as one who is willing to be blind. That is what is meant, I take it, by saying that I am responsible for my blindness. I cannot any longer, after the initial act of accepting it and the decision, renewed moment by moment, to live with it, ask to be regarded as someone to whom blindness has happened, as weathering happens to a rock. For I am not a rock but a man, and a man, not in spite of my disability, but within that disability. Freedom makes it possible for me to put to some use even what threatened to deprive me of all use: I can treat my blindness as an obstacle to be surmounted on the way to fresh achievement, not at all as a cul-de-sac.

What is true in this case is true in all cases. Hence it can be said that 'we have the war that we deserve', 'I am as profoundly responsible for it as if I had declared it myself.' 'I bear on my shoulders the weight of the whole world, without any person or thing being in a position to lighten the weight.'[1] It is here that the Jew reveals by his plight the situation in which we all are, but which we others are able to evade. 'To be a Jew is to be flung into, and *abandoned* in, the Jewish situation, and at the same time, to be responsible in and through one's own person for the destiny and the very nature of the Jewish people.'[2]

But a still more profound and exacting responsibility devolves upon us who are human. While I am free, I did not give myself freedom. I did not choose to

---

[1] *L'Être et le Néant*, 639.
[2] *Portrait of the Anti-Semite* (1948), 75.

be free. Yet I am responsible not only for the particular uses of my freedom, but for freedom itself. I will not allow anyone to enslave me, I am ashamed when someone excuses me for a fault on the ground that 'poor fellow, he could not help it!' I demand to be treated as a free person, even when it might seem more pleasant to be treated as a thing. Again, I did not bring myself into being, yet I am accountable for what I am. It is an affront to suggest that I am not. I insist on my rights as an Englishman, though I am an Englishman on quite different grounds from those on which I am an author or a tennis-player. If I claim the privileges that attend upon my being what I am, must I not also accept accountability for this?[1] Behind all my particular choices lies the choice of myself, of that project that is I. Such a choice did not precede my freedom, it *is* my freedom. The ground of my being is therefore something I did not originate, yet for which I am responsible. I am guilty by the mere fact of being in the world.

'I am responsible for everything in fact, except my responsibility itself, for I cannot be the ground of my own being. Everything then comes about as if I were forced to be responsible, I am *abandoned* in the world, not in the sense in which I should remain abandoned and passive in a hostile world like a plank floating on water. The sense is quite otherwise. All at once I find myself alone and with none to help me, committed in a

---

[1] It should be said that this interpretation of what it means to be responsible, particularly to be responsible for what one is, is my own and not Sartre's. But it seems to follow from his premises.

world for which I bear the entire responsibility, without my being able, even for an instant, to rid myself of this responsibility. For if I want to evade my responsibilities, I am responsible for such a desire. To play a passive part in the world, to refuse to act on other things and other people, is still to choose. Suicide is one out of several modes of being-in-the-world. Meanwhile, I encounter an absolute responsibility in the fact that my facticity, that is to say, in this case the fact of my birth, can never be apprehended directly and is indeed inconceivable. For my birth never appears to me a brute fact, but always through the medium of some projective reconstruction on the part of my *for-itself*. I am ashamed of being born, or I am surprised at it, or I am glad of it, or, in attempting to take away my life, I affirm that I live and I accept this state of things as evil. Thus, in a certain sense, I *choose* to be born.'[1]

Whatever criticisms one may be disposed to pass on so startling a conclusion, it has at least one great merit, inasmuch as it challenges the contemporary mood of irresponsibility, the couldn't-care-less attitude. It is clear that this ontology involves an ethic. It is indeed as the effort after a new morality that Sartre's existentialism must be judged.

(*f*)

At this point I am compelled to part company with most of the writers on Sartre known to me. For they tend either to deny that he has any ethic or to refuse him the right to have any. They dismiss his novels as so

[1] *L'Être et le Néant*, 641.

much 'black literature', seeing in them only a passion
for the obscene and the morbid, contempt for all that
lifts man above the animal, and an unqualified acceptance of the cynical maxim: *Homo homini lupus*. Or,
acknowledging that he is concerned with social justice
and a sworn foe to anti-Semitism, not to mention his
participation in the resistance movement, they ask in
amazement how one who sets out from his wholly
negative standpoint (as they see it) can arrive at such
conclusions. There is a gross misunderstanding here.
While I would not for a moment deny that there is
something unhealthy about the novels of Sartre, an
obsession with what nauseates, to use his own term,
his descriptions of the lusts and greeds and malice of
men and women are meant to be read not merely as an
account of what they are, but—on existentialist principles—of what they choose to be. Only when they see
what their inauthentic existence is can they be shamed
into revolt and the choice of authentic existence. It may
be said, of course, that Sartre should have made his
purpose more plain, should at any rate have pointed out
the better life the reader should choose. But the whole
previous exposition has failed if it has not made clear
that this is the one thing Sartre may not do. Values
must arise out of our freedom and not be taken over
from someone else. What the reader must do he will
find out for himself in the course of the experience of
reliving the characters in the novel. If he does not, if he
justifies his own inauthentic existence by that of the
characters in question, that is an abuse of his freedom
to destroy freedom for which he is responsible.

Man and his Freedom

That Sartre has an ethic should by now be beyond doubt. In *What is Literature?* he seems to some critics to go so far as virtually to subordinate literature, to social justice. In *Crime Passionel* he has exposed the internal tyrannies and the unscrupulousness of Communist parties, as in *The Respectable Prostitute* he has revealed the shameful inhumanity of the southern states in their treatment of the negro. One of the strongest protests against any kind of race-hatred is to be found in his *Portrait of the Anti-Semite*. It will suffice to quote here the conclusion of the book:

'No Frenchman will be free as long as the Jews do not enjoy their rights to the full. No Frenchman will be secure as long as a Jew, not only in France, but in the *world at large*, need go in fear of his life.'[1]

Again, what kind of ethic is in fact deduced from the analysis of the human situation in *L'Être et le Néant* may be seen best from the writings of Simone de Beauvoir. These are characterized by a hatred of oppression and a concern for human values that are wholly admirable. No one can fail to note the sensitive conscience at work in her discussion of the relation between ends and means or, even more, in her resolve to maintain the supremacy of morals over politics. In some respects, her best essay is the one in which she shows the morality concealed within the passion for revenge and how, when this has been replaced by the impersonal procedures of a court of law, the gain in justice is bought dearly by a loss of that intimate relation between an evil action and its punishment which

[1] *Op. cit.*, 128.

73

existed in the ruder methods of a more primitive society. It is clear that we have in her a writer for whom moral issues are of supreme importance, and for whom at the same time Sartre's philosophy appears not as *a* possible basis for such moral judgments as she reaches, but as *the one* possible basis for them.[1]

The standpoint of Sartre and his followers can be best described as an atheist humanism. It is however not always noticeably different, as far as can be seen at present, from the main Christian and liberal tradition of the West. One would have thought it cause for satisfaction among Christians that one who begins by denying God's existence and seeks to construct his morality *de novo* should in the end but confirm the wisdom of the centuries. That does not seem to be the attitude usually adopted, however. Instead, it is urged that there is something shamelessly illogical about the transition from *L'Être et le Néant* to *Portrait of the Anti-Semite*. How can the assertion of liberty be made to yield respect for the liberties of others? What link binds together 'Hell is . . . other people' and the ideals of liberty, equality, fraternity? In short, if man makes his own values, on what grounds can it be asserted that he ought to make these values and not others? How can there be moral obligation, when man himself is its sole source?

One reply that might legitimately be made is that a morality is surely to be judged by its content and not by

[1] See especially *Pour une Morale de l'Ambiguité* (1947), and *L'Existentialisme et la Sagesse des Nations* (1948). Berdyaev's essay on 'Sartre and the Future of Existentialism' in *Towards a New Epoch* (1949), 95ff. shows how he failed to grasp the connection between such an ethic and Sartre's novels.

Man and his Freedom

the arguments that seek to establish and justify it. In this sphere, the judge's ·dictum that one's verdict is likely to be right and the reasons given for it wrong, may well be valid. The connection between a general philosophy and an ethic is always a subtle one and seldom purely logical. The former can do no more than outline certain possibilities, the latter is an option from among these. And in the case of Sartre, to ask for a logical connection between his ontology and his ethics would be to require him to abandon his initial philosophical standpoint. If all values are the work of freedom and freedom is the emergence of that which cannot be accounted for in terms of what preceded it, if it is man transcending his past towards his future, there can in the nature of the case be no deduction of values from some given principles. Their justification is where their origin is, in freedom. In the last resort, Sartre should say that he has chosen certain values, set up certain standards, and that is all that can be said. To those who choose otherwise he would then have no answer.

It is to his credit as a moralist that he has not been content to do this. He has in fact offered a theoretical justification of morality itself and of the kind of morality he adopts. So doing, he has eased the position of his followers at the cost of his own consistency. As freedom is the source of all values, so it is their criterion. A course of action is to be approved that makes for the realization of freedom, to be disapproved if it militates against this. Thus, what Sartre terms 'the spirit of seriousness' is condemned mercilessly. He defines this as the attitude of mind for which there are certain values, fixed and given independently of ourselves, so that all we have to do is to recognize them and act accordingly. On closer examination, however, it turns out that he means rather an attitude of mind that accepts relative values as absolute and therefore beyond question, as when a Prussian officer cannot think except in the categories of his class or a devout Catholic commits his conscience to the Church for guidance. As against any such position, he is insistent that man must make his own standards. At the level of ordinary life, 'everything is permitted, since God is dead and we must die'.[1] But life cannot continue on this lack of basis. Since there is no God—and Sartre does not so much prove this as assume it—man must himself produce, manufacture, invent values. 'We have neither behind us, nor before us in a luminous realm of values, any means of justification or excuse.'[2] There is no world but the human world and man must introduce values into this or there will be none.[3] In the moment of illumination Orestes cries: 'From now on I'll take no one's orders, neither man's nor god's.' He continues:

'What a change has come over everything, and oh,

[1] *Situations* (1947), I, 103.
[2] *Existentialism and Humanism*, 34. Cf. p. 54: 'I am very sorry that it should be so, but if I have excluded God the Father, there must be somebody to invent values.' Here we see clearly the influence of Descartes, for whom God invents values in his absolute freedom.
[3] 'Since man is thus self-surpassing, and can grasp objects only in relation to his self-surpassing, he is himself the heart and centre of his transcendence. There is no other universe except the human universe, the universe of human subjectivity.' *Ibid.*, 55.

76

Man and his Freedom

how far away you seem! Until now I felt something warm and living round me, like a friendly presence. That something has just died. What emptiness! What endless emptiness, as far as eye can reach!'[1]

There is no God, and man is alone in an empty world. But it need not remain empty. He can fill it with content, and that is precisely what his duty is. Again and again Simone de Beauvoir argues that the very senselessness of human existence is the basis of morality. Just because our being here is absurd and void of significance, we can and should invest it with significance. If it had meaning of its own, why should we trouble to bring meaning into it? Indeed, could we do so? A world without values of its own is a world ready for man as a moral being who will create values and so give it what it would not have possessed without him. Existentialism, she says, is not a doctrine of despair. It is a message of hope. For it man is neither naturally good nor naturally bad. He is free, and he becomes good or bad according as he accepts his freedom or denies it.

'The separation of consciousnesses is a metaphysical fact, but man can rise above it. He can unite himself with other men across the world. Existentialists are so far from denying love, friendship, and brotherhood that for them it is only within these human relationships that each individual can find a basis for, and the fulfilment of, his being. But they do not consider these sentiments as given in advance. They have to be won. . . . Man is sole and sovereign master of his destiny if

[1] *The Flies* and *In Camera* (1946), 23.

77

Man and his Freedom

only he wills to be such. That is what existentialism affirms, and that is surely optimism.'[1]

We return to the fundamental assertion that man is what he chooses to be. What the novels and plays of Sartre describe is inauthentic existence, what a man chooses to be by the repudiation of his liberty. If this is possible, there is also the possibility of authentic existence, by which he chooses to live out and by his liberty. There is no need to import obligation into human life, it is the stuff of which it is made. To exist is to be obliged to be free: what is left to us is the way in which we will be free. And in the last resort there are just these two ways, to use our freedom against freedom or to use it for freedom. While I do not think that, strictly speaking, Sartre has the right to say more than that he chooses the second alternative and appeals to others to do the same, I am glad that he has in fact assumed a value independent of freedom that enables him to describe one exercise of freedom as right and the other as wrong. Authenticity is superior to inauthenticity. It 'consists in assuming a lucid and true awareness of the situation, in accepting the responsibilities and risks incurred in that situation, and in maintaining it in the moment of pride or of humiliation, and sometimes in the moment of abhorrence and hatred'.[2]

---

[1] *L'Existentialisme et la Sagesee des Nations*, 41f.

[2] *Portrait of the Anti-Semite*, 75f. Cf. Mathieu on the tower: 'I am through with remorse, with hesitations, with mental reservations. No one has the right to judge me; no one is thinking about me; no one can make up his mind for me. He had reached a decision without remorse, with full knowledge of the facts. . . . Here and now I have decided that death has all along been the secret of my life, that I have lived for the sole purpose of dying.' *The Iron in the Soul* (1950), 219f. It should perhaps be pointed out that in *L'Être et le*

78

Man and his Freedom

While there is much in Marjorie Grene's *Dreadful Freedom* with which I should be disposed to quarrel, I agree with her judgment that 'in such a situation, the ultimate value is honesty rather than freedom'. 'Existentialism is an ethic of *integrity*, in which running away from one's self is evil, facing one's self is good.'[1]

It must not be supposed that the choice for authentic against inauthentic existence is of the same order as the choice of one line of conduct rather than another. For it involves the whole self, and may best be described as a radical conversion. What that means can be seen in the case of Orestes in *The Flies*. To this we shall return later. Sartre seems to recognize here something akin to religious conversion, but differing from it by the fact that the radical change is wholly the work of the individual himself, who sees into his situation as never before, gives up what has hitherto been his *raison d'être*, dies as what he is and lives again as what he becomes.[2]

But is not this so much unbridled self-assertion merely? Not at all. For, as we have seen, liberty does not exist in a general way but only in concrete situations and in relation with other people who share those situations with us. Hence he who wills authentic existence will do so in concrete situations and in cooperation

Néant death does not play the decisive role Heidegger assigns to it. Death, Sartre would say, is not one of my possibilities, so that I can contemplate it in advance; it is the negation of all my possibilities and beyond my control. It does not give significance to life, but takes all significance from it. It is the triumph of the point of view of others over my own; as dead, I am reduced to a thing for them to observe. 'It was absurd that we were born, it is absurd that we shall die.' *Op. cit.*, 621ff.

[1] *Op. cit.*, 143f.

[2] Jeanson: *Le Problème Moral et la Pensée de Sartre*, 293ff.

with other persons. He will therefore be willing to undertake binding obligations, to enter a political party, to participate in the resistance movement, and so on. He is not giving up or restricting his liberty by so doing, he is exercising it, since his liberty is that of a Frenchman in the year 1942 with all that implies. He has all the freedom he can have under those circumstances, and that is all the freedom there is for him. Similarly, while it is true that in the condition of inauthenticity the other person is my rival against whom I am constantly on my guard, authenticity makes it possible for me to achieve a new relation, one of equality and friendship.

These two aspects of liberty—that it is always in particular historical conditions and that it only is as related to others who are also free—may be combined only if we identify ourselves with the effort that is being made in our day to bring liberty and true human status to the oppressed in our own and every land. Liberty is fully exercised only in the struggle for the liberation of others. This is well brought out by Simone de Beauvoir. She would say that to engage thus in the struggle for human liberty is to transcend the frustration to which all human effort is subject. True, our gain is never the final one, victory will be followed by defeat, the struggle is endless. But that is no reason for disheartenment. A certain zest and joy can be found in accepting this frustration and willing the good in it. And the good so achieved will not be relative, it will be absolute. Granted that the liberation of Paris only solved some problems in order to create others, the liberation was a good in itself and as such an occasion for unqualified rejoicing.[1] So it is possible to do what the religious moralist would describe as embodying eternal value in a passing moment.

It is unfortunate that Sartre has not left the vindication of existentialist morality to his able lieutenant but has entered the lists himself. His *Existentialism and Humanism* would not deserve to be taken seriously were it not the work of one who insists that we are wholly responsible for every action of ours and that no excuse may be admitted. The tone of the lecture is frivolous at many places and language is used that shows a lack of careful preparation. Perhaps the intention was to shock rather than to instruct. At any rate, he argues here that, while there is no human nature prior to our freedom or common to all men, there is a common human condition. In virtue of this:

'When we say that man chooses himself, we do mean that every one of us must choose himself; but by that we also mean that in choosing for himself he chooses for all men. For in effect, of all the actions a man may take in order to create himself as he wills to be, there is not one which is not creative, at the same time, of an image of man such as he believes he ought to be.'

'I am thus responsible for myself and for all men, and I am creating a certain image of man as I would have him be. In fashioning myself I fashion man.'

This seems to me a wholly artificial and forced argument. It is simply not true to say that 'what we choose

[1] *Pour une Morale de l'Ambiguité*, 175f.

is always the better; and nothing can be better for us unless it is better for all'.[1] This is only the case if we choose with full knowledge and entire integrity and unselfishness. There is much more force in Simone de Beauvoir's contention that we are free only in relation to others and that when we allow the other his liberty and cooperate with him we are in fact much more free than when we impose ourselves upon him to reduce him to a thing or act a part before him to ward off the danger from him. She is superior too in her appreciation of the difficulties of moral judgment in concrete situations. Granted that we must not use means that would defeat our ends, there are times when we can only achieve our ends by temporarily abandoning them. The statesman is constantly faced with dilemmas of this kind. His morality is one of ambiguity. Is he to relax the divorce law and relieve private suffering at the expense of social stability, or *vice versa*? Is he to defend international law by laying waste a country and massacring its people or to preserve human lives by allowing aggression to triumph? Whichever course he adopts, he has no guarantee that the end envisaged will in fact be reached. He only spotlights the common human situation by his dreadful uncertainties. The human situation as such is ambiguous: man knows himself as subject, but the material universe destroys him as mere object; he wants to eternalize his life but must die, he lives in the present but it slips through his fingers as he contemplates it, he does not know whether he is a sovereign individual or a mere unit in

[1] *Existentialism and Humanism*, 29f.

the mass. But he can live bravely in face of this ambiguity, accepting the responsibility for decisions reached in the half-light that alone is given to him, neither over-elated with success nor unduly depressed by failure. In all circumstances he can show himself a man.

Criticism of this position will be reserved till later. It is enough now to point out that it is not without nobility, and that it is a welcome antidote to the widespread sense of futility that does so much harm today.

(g)

It may lend interest to this discussion if we pause to consider here how some of Sartre's ideas are worked out in two of his plays and in a novel by Camus.

Crime Passionel is one of his best-known plays, and the fact that it is concerned with the intrigues within a Communist party makes it of special and topical interest. Hugo is a young man of bourgeois origin who has joined the Party, very largely as an act of rebellion against his father. He is the typical intellectual and the weakness of his type is brought out sharply by the hesitations and inner conflict into which he is thrown when sent by the committee to murder Hoederer, one of the leaders of the Proletarian Party. He toys with the idea of killing him but always finds some excuse to prevent himself from acting. Hoederer is by contrast the man of resolution, above scruples, the born leader who does not shrink from committing others as well as himself. Hence the spell he casts over Hugo and also over Jessica, the latter's wife, who finds herself thrown without warning into the intrigues and perils from which she had always been so carefully shielded. When Hugo shoots Hoederer, it is because he finds Jessica in his arms; the act is one of impulse and passion, not at all of decision. But in the closing scene of the play, when he has been released from prison only to find that meantime the Party had gone over to Hoederer's policy, he passes his motives in review. Did he kill Hoederer in a moment of passion merely or was it also because he regarded his policy as a betrayal of the ideals with which he joined the Party? As he looks back, he is not able to disentangle the two sets of motives. But he can assume his action now for the right motive. 'I don't know why I killed Hoederer, but I know why I should have killed him; because he was following a bad policy, because he lied to his comrades and because through him the Party might have become rotten.' Now, in face of death, he identifies himself with his action as a political one entirely and by so doing makes it such. 'A man like Hoederer doesn't die by accident. He dies for his ideals, for his policy, he is responsible for his own death. If I recognize my crime before you all, if I reclaim my name of Raskolnikov, if I agree to pay the necessary price, then he will have had the death he deserved.'[1] So the intellectual transcends his old wavering and self-analysis and wins through to the decision by which he makes, not his acts only, but his very self.

The second play is *The Flies*, a modern version of the story of Orestes and Electra. Orestes arrives in Argos

[1] *Three Plays* (1945), 105f.

Man and his Freedom

from Corinth, where he has been brought up since his father's murder. He travels with his tutor, who has made of him a man without attachments:

'Along with youth, good looks and wealth, you have the wisdom of far riper years; your mind is free from prejudice and superstition, you have no family ties, no religion, and no calling; you are free to turn your hand to anything. But you know better than to commit yourself—and there lies your strength. So, in a word, you stand head and shoulders above the ruck and, what's more, you could hold a chair of philosophy or architecture in a great university!'[1]

When he meets Electra, he does not betray his identity, and is disturbed by the passion for revenge that dominates all her thoughts. She lives for the return of her brother and the vengeance he will execute. When they meet again, he reveals himself and begs her to come away with him to Corinth. Her indignant refusal of the suggestion reveals to him how rootless he is; there has been no purpose in his life. 'The solid passions of the living were never mine.' Even in Argos there is no place for him, he belongs nowhere. What is he to do? He appeals to Zeus to give a sign. A miracle bids him submit and do what is right. But something in him revolts, he undergoes an existentialist conversion, repudiating the standards that are offered to him and making his own in their place. He will act, he will take upon himself the dread responsibility of murder and so free Argos from the remorse by which it is haunted. Zeus intervenes to save Aegisthus by getting

[1] *The Flies* and *In Camera*, 20.

85

him to arrest Orestes, and in the dialogue between them the representatives of order face together the fact of human freedom.

'*Zeus.* Each keeps order; you in Argos, I in heaven and on earth—and you and I harbour the same dark secret in our hearts.

Aegisthus. I have no secret.

Zeus. You have. The same as mine. The bane of gods and kings. The bitterness of knowing men are free.'[1]

'Why do you not destroy Orestes yourself?' the king asks. The god replies: 'Once freedom lights its beacon in a man's heart, the gods are powerless against him.'[2] So he is allowed to take his course.

Orestes murders his mother and her paramour. But when the deed is done, Zeus tempts him and his sister with the throne of Argos in return for remorse. Let them disown their act as evil, as against the order of the universe, and spend the rest of their lives in penitence for it. Electra succumbs but Orestes resists and maintains his integrity to the end by acknowledging his act, without shame or regret, as his own and therefore right.

'Yesterday, when I was with Electra, I felt at one with Nature, this Nature of your making. It sang the praises of the Good—*your* Good—in siren tones. . . . Suddenly, out of the blue, freedom crashed down on me and swept me off my feet. Nature sprang back, my youth went with the wind, and I knew myself alone, utterly alone in the midst of this well-meaning little

[1] *Ibid.*, 72.
[2] *Ibid.*, 74.

universe of yours. I was like a man who's lost his
shadow. And there was nothing left in heaven, no
Right or Wrong, nor anyone to give me orders.'[1]

Judged by the standards of freedom, the murder was
a meritorious act because Orestes chose it as the
expression of himself; to repent of it afterwards would
have been evil, since that would be the surrender of
one's own values to those of tradition, society, and
religion. To be fair to Sartre, one should make allow-
ance for the fact that the murder is a given element in
the story; there is no glorification of matricide but only
of freedom.

In an earlier novel, *The Outsider*, Albert Camus had
depicted the man whose whole attitude to life is one of
non-attachment; he takes pleasure where he can find it,
but is unwilling for any binding relations to other
persons. He looks from the outside on all that happens
and shoots a man under what may be a touch of sun-
stroke. Even the prospect of death only rouses him to
a passionate outburst, it does not awake genuine selfhood in him. Sartre describes the book as a 'novel of
the absurd'.[2] The theme of *The Plague* is in marked
contrast to this. A town in North Africa is struck by
plague and in consequence is isolated from the world
outside. It thus becomes a symbol of the human situation, with the threat of inescapable death overhanging
us at every moment. We are shown various reactions
to what is going on within the city. One exploits it for
his own gain, another yearns for the woman he loves,

[1] *Ibid.*, 96.
[2] *Situations*, I, 99ff.

a third is active in fighting the plague, though his ideal is merely negative, to do nothing that will increase the sum-total of evil in the world. Two men stand out above the rest. One is the priest, who tries in his sermons to justify the ways of God with men even under such circumstances and finally calls for blind submission. The other is the doctor. He refuses to justify the unjustifiable. An atheist, he faces the plague as a grim horror with which he contends to the utmost, regardless of his own happiness. When the plague ebbs away and he sees others returning to the common life that cannot again be his, since his wife has died elsewhere in a sanatorium during this period of conflict, he tells himself that 'it was only right that those whose desires are limited to man and his humble yet formidable love, should enter, if only now and again, into their reward'. The doctor himself embodies and ennobles 'the never-ending fight against terror and its relentless onslaughts, despite their personal afflictions, by all who, unable to be saints but refusing to bow down to pestilences, strive their utmost to be healers'.[1] So we arrive at an atheist humanism, for which man's vocation is to redeem for a little while what is finally beyond redemption. For who can say that the plague will not return?

(h)

In what precedes I have been concerned to give as fair a presentation of Sartre's philosophy as possible, and in particular to defend it against certain misunder-

---

[1] *The Plague* (1948), 277, 284.

standings. I hope I have shown that it is not to be charged with nihilism or solipsism, but is a real effort to afford moral guidance for an age in which values are threatened and men have lost the traditional authorities that once directed their lives. There are, however, certain serious charges to be brought against it even by one who is anxious to do it justice.

1. I would repeat here what was said of Heidegger, that the world in which he operates is avowedly a man-made and therefore an artificial world. That everything in it is relative to man is a truism, since nothing can be known by us save under the conditions implied in knowledge, one of them being that it should be known by *us*. But a waterfall or a landscape are not relative to human life in the same way as a newspaper or a motor-cycle. Indeed, to treat a waterfall as merely a source of power for a factory and a landscape as no more than a building site is, we all feel, to do them injury. The values they have for us are of a different order from those we seek to impose upon them; their beauty may not be independent of our minds, but it is more independent than their utility. It is something that belongs to them and is entitled to our recognition and even respect. If natural objects are not *for-themselves* as persons are, they are not *in-themselves* quite as things are. Martin Buber is therefore right when he places our life with nature in what he calls 'the world of relation'; there is something about it of an I-Thou relation.[1]

2. Equally serious is the omission of children. The

[1] *I and Thou* (1937), 6. This is of course much more the case with animals.

world of Sartre is, with one or two slight exceptions, peopled with adults, and with very sophisticated adults at that. This leads to the omission from his analysis of the human situation of some of the most important elements in it. For example, he regards freedom as irrupting ready-made into the world, whereas it is rather something that has to be elicited by freedom in others. Would the child pass from impulse to self-transcendence and far-reaching decision if he were not trained thereto by the society into which he is born, by the home in the first instance? Again, as with Heidegger, the failure to notice even the mystery of birth leaves him insensitive to the sacred as a dimension of human life. The child comes to us, not as an accident, but as a gift and trust. It is in his presence that perhaps we realize most acutely what it means to be under moral obligation. For here there is nothing whatever to restrict the exercise of physical power and yet we feel such restraints upon that power as obtain nowhere else. The very helplessness of the child commands our reverence. I doubt whether under such circumstances anyone can actually judge that human life, this life that is before him, is absurd, unjustifiable, and without value save as he himself confers value upon it.

3. There is in Sartre the same misrepresentation of the all-important distinction between authenticity and inauthenticity that we found in Heidegger. No doubt, for the purposes of philosophical discussion, they have to be distinguished sharply as two opposing possibilities, like the closed society and the open society in Bergson's *The Two Sources of Morality and Religion*. But

these types are constructions and not actualities: all actual existence is mixed. So, for the purposes of the drama, it may well be necessary to present the two types of existence as two successive stages in the development of a character, and to mark the passage from the one to the other, as in the case of Orestes discussed in the previous section. But human life as we know it from within is neither inauthentic nor authentic wholly. It has its shames and its splendours, its baseness and its nobility, at every moment. Where the novels of Sartre are so misleading is that we read them as descriptions of life, whereas they are descriptions rather of life in so far as it is lived inauthentically. Like Heidegger, he has emptied the daily intercourse between men of all moral content in order that he may be able to introduce this later by a *tour de force* of his own.

4. While Sartre's philosophy presents itself to us as an assertion and vindication of freedom, it is not itself a work of freedom. The mind behind it is not an open one, but is governed by dogmas. The first of those dogmas is the non-existence of God. I have not found in Sartre's writings any argument against God's existence that does not take for granted what has to be proved. Marjorie Grene restates the argument as a demonstration that the concept of one who is *causa sui* is self-contradictory.[1] But that turns upon the elementary blunder of supposing that terms used of God are to be understood, not only in the sense in which they are used of man, but also in the sense in which they are used of man as he would be were there no God! One

[1] *Dreadful Freedom*, 42.

Man and his Freedom

has the right to expect something better than that from a professional philosopher.

The denial of God leads him to the position in which he is bound to describe human life as absurd because we are responsible for ourselves while we did not bring ourselves into being. The word 'responsible' in this connection must be understood, I take it, in the sense that we hold ourselves responsible and not merely that other people call us to account. I cannot, however, see how responsibility is possible unless there is some tribunal beyond ourselves by which we know ourselves to be judged. My responsibility must be 'before' something or someone: it cannot be self-made. It would seem therefore that the facts to which Sartre appeals—the sheer givenness of my being-in-the-world and my sense of responsibility not only for what I do but even for what I am—can be accounted for more simply. Do they not suggest that I am no mere accident, that I have been given to myself, that my life is a trust from God and that I am responsible to him for the use to which I put it? If we must have mythical language, does not the inescapable sense of responsibility suggest that we have been sent here, rather than that we have been thrown down and abandoned? Each human self is constituted, not by a choice, but by what lies deeper than choice, by a divine overture and its response thereto. 'It is he that hath made us, and we are his.'

One serious consequence of the atheist dogma is that morality is restricted to what arises out of a deliberate choice. There is therefore no room in it for the

Man and his Freedom

graces of the good life alongside of its achievements. These can, of course, arise only where the good life is something received as well as something attained. Such fruits of the spirit as humility and gratitude, peace and joy belong to it equally with courage, justice, and self-denial. There should be a radiance about it as well as a resolution. The N.T. ethic of love and the leading of the Spirit, the fulfilment of the law because it is the deepest desire of the man made new in Christ, utter devotion to a person as response to an incredible deliverance—these introduce a dimension of morality that is lacking in Sartre, and must be, since God is absent and man is his own saviour.

The only justification that I can see for the atheist starting-point is the assumption, found also in Nicolai Hartmann, that God's purpose and man's freedom are mutually incompatible. God must be repudiated that morality may be possible.[1] To understand Sartre's position here, we must recall the significance for him of the other person's look. To know oneself observed is to lose one's status as a person and to be reduced to a thing. That would particularly be the case were there God, for his look would be absolutely inescapable. Before him, the omniscient and the omnipotent, man is without defence. He is driven therefore to see himself through God's eyes, to renounce responsibility for his own life and accept the part God designs him to play. That is brought out in the account Daniel gives

[1] 'That anything whatsoever in heaven or on the earth, even though it be God himself, should take precedence of man, would be ethically perverted; it would not be moral; it would be treason to mankind, which must rely upon itself alone.' *Ethics* (1932), III, 264.

93

to Mathieu of his conversion, a conversion shown by what follows to be a superficial and temporary affair, a surrender from which he recovers without achieving authenticity.

'I need no longer bear the responsibility of my turbid and disintegrating self: he who sees me causes me to be: I am as he sees me. I turn my eternal shadowed face towards the night. I stand up like a challenge, and I say to God: Here am I. Here am I, as you see me, as I am.'[1]

There is here a misunderstanding of the relation between God and man that has, it must be admitted, been shared by many Christians. My relation to God is such that it does not impair my freedom but grounds and enhances it. To be under God's eye is to be constituted a person, not to be reduced to a thing. As Jaspers has expressed it:

'The man who attains true awareness of his freedom gains certainty of God. Freedom and God are inseparable. Why?

'This I know: in my freedom I am not through myself, but am given to myself, for I can fail myself and I cannot force my freedom. Where I am authentically myself, I am certain that I am not through myself. The highest freedom is experienced in freedom from the world, and this freedom is a profound bond with transcendence.'[2]

5. The second dogma is the finality of death. The possibility that death may not be the end is simply not

[1] *The Reprieve* (1947), 364.
[2] *Way to Wisdom* (1951), 45.

considered. It is assumed that death is absurd, that it brings life to a close without rounding it off, and so on. I would not oppose to this dogma any equally dogmatic assertion of immortality, but would be content to plead that there is no justification whatever for approaching so momentous an event as death with a closed mind. The philosophical attitude is surely better expressed in the *Apology*, where Socrates ventures bravely into the unknown as one who will discover what lies within it in the only way in which such discovery is possible. It may be indeed that the possibility of life after death is not independent of the attitude in which we confront death, that hope and courage may win or find another life while the acceptance of this life as final would preclude one from that other. I do not suggest that this is so, but wish simply to point out that dogmatic denial is as little justified in this matter as dogmatic affirmation. Throughout, Sartre has in mind one's own death rather than the death of another; but it is this latter that invades our present experience with questioning and mystery.

6. What is meant in this type of existentialism by the creation of values is not at all clear. While Sartre speaks at times as though it were a wholly novel decision by which entirely fresh standards are produced *ex nihilo*, at other times one gets the impression that all that is meant is that we do not take over standards ready-made but only when and in so far as they have authenticated themselves to us. Most of us would accept the latter position as our own, but not the former. When he describes a young Frenchman during

the war as deciding whether to escape and join the Free French Forces or stay with his mother, he rightly says that no existing system of morality can solve his problem for him, he must solve it for himself. But in such a situation he does not create values, he is faced with two sets of claims which conflict and exercises not merely his freedom but his moral insight in deciding which claim to follow.[1]

Again, when Mathieu breaks through to freedom in the last minutes of his life, he does not create any new values, he merely does his duty as a soldier.[2] The invention of values turns out to be no more than a case of 'my station and its duties'. Not that I would reproach Sartre when the mountain of invention brings forth what resembles the mouse of convention. There seems to be little connection between the bold assertion that wholly new standards must be manufactured and the standards that are actually produced. And we may be glad that this is so. Hitler has shown what a man is likely to do when he really sets out to invent values, and it is to Sartre's credit that he takes so different a way. Is it that the theory is prompted by pride,[3] while the practice is inspired by humanity?

---

[1] *Existentialism and Humanism*, 35ff.

[2] 'He fired, and the tables of the Law crashed about him—Thou Shalt Love Thy Neighbour as Thyself—bang! in that bugger's face—Thou Shalt Not Kill—bang! at that scarecrow opposite. He was firing on his fellow men, on Virtue, on the whole world. Liberty is Terror. The mairie was ablaze, his head was ablaze. The world is going up in smoke, and me with it. . . . But Mathieu went on firing. He fired. He was cleansed. He was all-powerful. He was free.' *The Iron in the Soul*, 245.

[3] 'The self must assume its situation with the proud consciousness of being its author.' *L'Être et le Néant*, 639.

Man and his Freedom

7. While there is much in the examples of atheist humanism described in the previous section that commands our admiration, the very fact that their setting is a God-less one precludes certain possibilities, particularly those of repentance and forgiveness. It would seem indeed that Sartre does not distinguish between repentance and remorse. Thus, Orestes must either look back upon the murder of his mother without the least suggestion of shame or regret or he must allow himself to be demoralized and subdued (as Electra is) by pangs of conscience. But to assume one's past does not necessarily mean to approve it. I assume my past when I acknowledge it as my own act, defend it where I judge it to be right and make reparation for it where I now see it to have been mistaken. The prodigal son in the parable did not pretend that misery had come upon him otherwise than by his own folly. He had sinned against heaven and in his father's sight and he came home as one who had confessedly betrayed the trust placed in him. But equally he did not allow himself to become the victim of remorse; he willed to make such atonement for the past as was in his power. He could not ask to be received back as a son, but as a hired servant he would take whatever opportunity came to him to prove his worth. Repentance is just such a reckoning with the past before God; it is an act of freedom and utter honesty, when we judge ourselves more severely than our fellows would ever judge us and resolve to put right what has been done wrong, as far as is within our power. Such repentance can be met by forgiveness, as in the parable. Man as Sartre

describes him cannot be forgiven; indeed he does not need to be forgiven, because by accepting his acts in the past as the work of his freedom he puts them beyond it. Freedom turns to good everything it touches. But does it? May not freedom sometimes need to recognize guilt and burn with shame for it?

Forgiveness, of course, is not possible from God to man where God does not exist. I doubt whether for Sartre it is possible between man and man. For he would say that we dishonour the other when we treat him as in any sense the victim of circumstances and not as one who creates himself from moment to moment by his own freedom. But it is not necessary to find excuses of this kind for another before one forgives him. The reasons put forward by the spirit of charity are not really the motives for charity, they are the justification it offers after it has resolved to forgive. It is possible to 'forgive wrongs darker than death or night', because we see ourselves before God and know that, since all need forgiveness from him, none of us may refuse it to his brother.

To sum up. Sartre's world, whether for description or for action, is a sadly reduced world. It lacks the dimension of the holy. Man abandoned to himself is not truly man.

4. Reason, History, and Faith

THE relation in which the thought of Karl Jaspers stands to the main tradition of Western philosophy may be expressed in two ways.

In the first place, he has stated the three conditions for a profitable study of philosophy. They are (*a*) *participation in scientific inquiry*.[1] Originally, we may say, philosophy was a total knowledge within which the various scientific disciplines were included; at a later stage, they detached themselves one by one and became independent; now, while philosophy is not to be confused with science, it may not be practised fruitfully without science. It must learn from the scientific temper even while it transcends scientific results. (*b*) *The study of great philosophers*. Here the word 'great' is to be noted. The student must not lose himself in a maze of theories and counter-theories, he must make firsthand acquaintance with some master of thought. While existentialism therefore represents a new departure in philosophy, it does not break with tradition. Rather does it discover new values therein as it interprets, say, the Hegelian system as something more than

[1] *Way to Wisdom* (1951), 168f.

99

a system, as the expression of an insight. (*c*) *A conscien-tious approach to the conduct of daily life.* This third point is a new and challenging one. Truth in philosophy is truth that must be incorporated into life; equally, we arrive at truth of this order by personal decision and commitment and not by reflection only. We reach by these three methods a personal appropriation of what has come down from the past, an appropriation to be made in life as well as in thought.

In the second place, Jaspers aims at a renewal of the Western philosophical tradition by the incorporation into it of the distinctive insights of Kierkegaard and Nietzsche. While he accepts the results of neither of these, he is indebted to the methods of them both. They had a strange prevision of our situation, they raise for us the problems we must face and do not allow us to evade them. What is of most value in them is their passion for sincerity, their return to the origins of philosophy at a time when it was in danger of surrendering to the sciences, and their re-establishment of the lost connection between thought and life. Here we reach the same result as by the first path.[1]

In what follows I shall not repeat what I have written elsewhere, drawing there principally on the three volumes of the *Philosophie*.[2] I propose instead to deal briefly with some of the post-war developments in Jaspers's thinking, concentrating especially on four points. These are (*a*) his vindication of reason, (*b*) his

[1] 'The Importance of Nietzsche, Marx, and Kierkegaard' in *The Hibbert Journal* for April 1951.
[2] *The Self and its Hazards* (1950).

view of history and its meaning, (c) his 'natural theology', if one may use such a term for his ideas on God's existence and our relation to him, and (d) his attitude to Christianity. Some of the earlier themes will, of course, recur, but they will have undergone enrichment by the experiences through which the philosopher and we have passed in the war-years.

(a)

To accuse Jaspers of irrationalism is to demonstrate that one has not seriously attempted to understand him. His training was in science in the first instance, in medicine, and he practised in the psychotherapeutic clinic attached to the university faculty of medicine in Heidelberg before he went over to philosophy. As early as 1933, in a series of lectures delivered at Groningen, he had shown his resolve to maintain the balance as between reason and existence.[1] Now, indeed, he goes beyond that and tells us that he would give precedence to reason. He did not mean, by philosophy of existence, a new pattern of thinking, but simply the revival of 'the one, eternal philosophy', which needs to be rescued, as Kierkegaard sought to rescue it, from that slavery to the objective into which it had fallen in the course of last century. Today, however, he would employ the term reason to make clear this continuity he seeks to achieve with the past. For reason is at once the inspiration and the task of all genuine philosophy.[2]

[1] *Vernunft und Existenz.*
[2] *Vernunft und Widervernunft in unserer Zeit* (1950), 49f.

Our generation suffers from insecurity, and so is tempted to look for certainty where this cannot be found. We long for a system of knowledge, complete and final, that will shelter us; we would gladly resign our freedom to an authority that will guarantee our safety. In the past, we might have looked to religion or philosophy for such an authority, but today only science enjoys the prestige that once was theirs. Hence the appeal of two systems of thought that claim to be both science and more than science, Marxism and Freudian psycho-analysis. Each has made a valuable contribution to our knowledge of man and his situation, but neither would have attained the position it has today by this means only. Each also claims to be a total knowledge, a final answer to the problems of human life; each claims faith for itself. Worse still, each is an expression of the will to power, for each would enable a few men to manipulate their fellows, whether in the mass or as individuals. Each resorts to magic and sophistry; it has a whole series of formulae that are supposed to work like incantations dispelling all human ills, and any number of specious arguments by which to justify its every twist and turn. Because they acknowledge no God, they are arrogant and tyrannical, setting up orthodoxies that brand as traitors any who dare to be free enough to dissent.

These gross abuses of science should force us to reflect on what science is and what it is not. We either worship it because we mistake it for philosophy and religion, or we turn from it in disgust because we confuse it with mere technology, the expression of modern man's will to power. But science as its great practitioners understood it is neither one nor the other. It is less than philosophy but more than knowledge. It exists only in the form of the various sciences, each of these being knowledge of a certain class of objects, a knowledge gained by the employment of appropriate methods and from a particular standpoint. As such, it purchases its accuracy at the expense of adequacy; it can be confident of its results, because they refer only to certain aspects of our experience. But it arises in the first instance out of the disinterested will to truth. Man wants to know and will admit no limits to this enterprise. As he engages in it, however, he discovers that limits do exist, that there is a realm into which he cannot enter by means of his methods and in which no describable and measurable objects wait for his observation. Hence arises a genuine dissatisfaction with science and an aspiration after what transcends it.

But how do we enter into this region that lies beyond science? Is it the home merely of the irrational or is knowledge of another order possible within it? If we take the second alternative, a philosophy is conceivable that does justice both to existence and to reason. Before explaining what this means, it may be as well to indicate briefly what Jaspers means by existence. For him, as for Heidegger and Sartre, it stands for a possibility rather than a fact; my existence is what I have it in me to become, what is open to my freedom, what may be won or—by the repudiation of freedom—lost. It is the self, not as something given, but as something to be achieved. It can never become an object of knowledge, because it is always on the side of the subject. It is what is most certain in me yet what is most in peril; what I have received as a trust yet have to win ever again; by it I am involved in the world and with other selves yet am free to shape my own destiny. It is as such a self that I enter the realm that lies beyond the farthest point that knowledge of objects can reach; but I do not truly enter it unless I have traversed the area in which such knowledge is valid and experienced the wonder that comes when its boundary is reached and yet there is a beyond. The proposition that there is that which transcends science is not the foundation of philosophy; for this an actual encounter with the Transcendent is necessary.

We can now approach the relation between existence and reason. The one enters into the realm of mystery in faith, hope, and courage, the other consolidates what has been so won. The one gives life a content, the other gives that content form. Yet they are not two separate faculties or activities, they are two aspects of one activity in which the whole self is engaged. So a traveller ventures forward into a new country, exploring each stretch of land as he comes to it and marking down on a map what he finds. Without the venture the map would be so much blank paper, without the map-making no gains would accrue from the venture. We will allow Jaspers to express himself on this point:

'Reason creates the thought-space into which what is can be taken up, can be expressed in language that does justice to its unique nature, and so win validity.

This space within which reason operates might be compared to water, air, and light in which all life can grow, but which just on that account craves to be filled by such life, though always under the condition that it will allow itself to be permeated by reason.

To put the same thing in other words: Reason illuminates the Unconditioned but does not produce any content itself. It brings the forms that need to be filled if they are to become real in time. It understands historicity but is essentially not itself historical. It creates a space for the Unconditioned that gives content to existence.'[1]

Philosophizing is therefore the unity of existence and reason, and what this means can perhaps be seen best of all by examining a concrete instance of philosophizing. We may take the last hours of Socrates. There we see a man face to face with death and accepting with courage what it brings; he will enter the unknown, prepared for whatever it may contain. But this resolution in face of death expresses itself in the arguments of the *Phaedo*, whereby he orders, clarifies, and defends the original personal conviction that rules him. He uses the logic and the concepts appropriate to the objects of scientific knowledge, but always with a sense that they are no longer applicable, their meaning must be strained, they must be read as signs to what is inexpressible by them. The discourses of Epictetus and Boethius's *Consolations of Philosophy* are other instances of the same pattern of thinking, rational in form but deriving their substance from the profoundest personal

[1] *Vernunft und Widervernunft* etc., 46.

experiences. We must use Kant's language and say that they are works of *Vernunft* and not of *Verstand*.[1]

Existence as the venture of freedom makes possible a philosophy that is quite other than science, reason so uses what existence offers that it creates a philosophy that need not be ashamed before science. For it too is objective and lifted above the individual to the universal—though in its own way, of course. We may now briefly characterize reason as Jaspers understands it.

(*a*) Reason is *openness*. It is receptive of all truth, from whatever source it may come; it has no preconceptions that might decide in advance what can and what cannot happen. It does not exclude even what seems alien to it, the lonely destiny of such an exception to the common human lot as a Kierkegaard or Nietzsche and the claims of tradition and authority. It seeks to understand even where it must reject; itself order, it is capable of appreciating that chance and disorder have their part to play. Hence, while it retains what it has already won, it never does so in blindness to the new that challenges it.

(*b*) Reason is *clarity*. It is not satisfied, as the artist may be, with the suggestive and the mysterious; it accepts them as regions to be explored. Without reducing the Transcendent to a collection of objects, it throws upon it a light of inquiry that illuminates it and makes possible the appropriate degree of insight and

---

[1] We might include here Jaspers's discussion of the immediate problems of post-war Germany in *Die Schuldfrage*. In reading such a book one gains an insight into the soul of the writer, yet one is struck at the same time by the effort to set everything in the clear light of reason, the self-criticism, and the horror of even the slightest exaggeration in favour of his own position.

appreciation. It is the sworn enemy of all wishful thinking, and as such is on the watch against the danger that our encounter with the Transcendent may reflect ourselves rather than it.

(c) Reason is *the will to unity*. It is not satisfied with a mere series of insights, however great the significance they severally yield; it must test them by one another, ask how they cohere, and seek to weld them into a unified whole. It knows that a system can never be adequate to experience, therefore it refuses to recognize as absolute any actual unity it may achieve, for this will be only temporary and partial; yet it cannot surrender the faith that there is that by which our life may be unified. 'To be able to seek the One the seeker must himself become one.'[1] The final unity in things may be apprehended only existentially and not intellectually.

(d) Reason *uses the methods and categories of understanding in order to transcend them*. We are imprisoned within the subject-object dichotomy, so that we can only think and speak of objects. Even when we think of the subject, we turn it thereby into something else, a special kind of object, while what does the thinking and therefore alone has claim to the status of subject is *ipso facto* excluded. Hence, when we refer to what cannot be an object, we must use concepts as signs and statements as pointers to what cannot be stated. It is here that an acute difficulty arises, for reason is thus in danger of being misunderstood. There are those who confuse it (*Vernunft*) with understanding (*Verstand*)

[1] *Ibid.*, 35.

and either reduce philosophy to a special discipline like one of the sciences, making it, for example, logic or the study of language, or abandon it altogether as useless when they find it cannot be so reduced. On the other hand, there are those who, disillusioned with science once they discover its limitations, turn from it and philosophy alike to the irrational, to ideology or the worship of a leader. Against both errors we must maintain the worth of the philosopher's task and his right to pursue it. While the only map he can construct is on a plane surface, what he refers to by means of this is something quite different, a global being that is authenticated for us by the fact that we ourselves belong to it.

(e) Reason is *in communication.* It can never be satisfied with a merely private experience, but must share with others and learn from others. Because it dare not confer absolute value on what it has won, it seeks correction and enrichment by the insights of others. It is not sure that anything has been fully appropriated by itself save as it can throw it into a form in which it can be apprehended by another. 'It is not I who bring the truth, but I seek it with the man with whom I have to do, I seek it as one who listens, questions, and attempts.' 'If God is eternal, truth exists for us men in time as the truth that comes about through communication.'[1] The intercourse of free and open minds is the one sure way to truth, and it is so indispensable that we must never admit that it is no longer possible. Even where the other party to a conversation uses a different

[1] *Ibid.,* 36.

Reason, History, and Faith

language from our own, we must still seek tirelessly to find or to create a common language.

What has been said so far might suggest, though the suggestion was repudiated at the outset, that reason is a special faculty of some kind. It is not. It is of the same order as existence inasmuch as it is possibility rather than actuality. 'Reason is not there by nature, but is only real through a resolution.'[1] It is an attitude that a man takes up and in which he persists in face of all that threatens it. Since he comes to reason only through a resolution, something of a conversion is implied, and Plato said as much in the *Republic*. He ventures upon reason in the act by which he dares to be free, to seek truth at any cost to himself, to be whole and sincere, to live by what is absolute. He does this by no development but by a free resolve that is at once his own act and a revelation of what lies at the foundation of his being. As in the Bible, he is born from above and yet he turns himself about.

Once this new life has been entered on, it brings its fears and dangers. It is senseless to ask: Will truth prevail? The only question that has meaning runs: What can I do for the victory of truth? Truth has power independently of me, otherwise it would not win my allegiance; yet it can only be a power in the world as I serve it. And perhaps I can best serve truth when I am powerless, for otherwise I shall be in danger of enlisting it in the service of my own interests and claims. Across the centuries therefore I salute 'the long line of men of thought from Thales to the present day, men

[1] *Ibid.*, 41.

109

individually powerless, but ultimately the rulers of the world'.[1]

We live in a day when the future is dreadfully obscure. We have witnessed so many triumphs of error and evil within history that we shudder at the prospect that history may even end in an Armageddon in which the victory goes to the forces of darkness. But reason as we have described it is not without hope. As it discerns the eternal in the temporal, so it can glimpse the possibility that the eternal may triumph though the temporal fall in ruin. While there is a world, it can labour to transmute loss into gain with a power like that of love.

As I see it, it is one of the major achievements of Jaspers that he incorporates into his philosophy the subjective emphasis of Kierkegaard without losing the tradition of objectivity. If there is a universal that offers itself, as in the natural sciences, to be apprehended by all minds in the same way, so there is another that offers itself to all persons to be apprehended by each in his own way. It is true, of course, that the expression of this universal is not the privilege of philosophy. It may be urged that art is better qualified for this, especially if it is enlisted in the service of religion. Indeed, are there not mysteries so profound that they can only be received and communicated in awed silence? But the philosopher cannot adopt these methods, because his vocation is to express in clear, logical form whatever he deals with, even when in the nature of the case it is distorted by being presented in this form. If he bears

[1] A. N. Whitehead: *Science and the Modern World* (1927), 260.

Reason, History, and Faith

the distortion always in mind, it need not bar him from achieving a metaphysic, though it will not be a system like that of Hegel, it will be a tentative reading of the signs by which the Godhead communicates with us.[1]

(b)

Of the contemporary existentialists, Berdyaev and Jaspers are the only ones to concern themselves with the problem of history and its meaning, though Heidegger, it is true, has a section on the subject in

[1] This seems the point at which to draw attention to some of the gross errors in Bobbio: *The Philosophy of Decadentism*.

Page 16: He speaks of 'the self-centred existence of Jaspers', when the latter in fact labours to show how we can only find ourselves as we give ourselves away, to other persons, to concrete tasks in the world, and to the Transcendent.

Page 19: Of 'the metaphysics of Jaspers, understood as a reading of the cipher language of transcendency', it is said that 'the more deluded and fanciful it is, the more certain is it of being in the way of truth'. Whereas he emphasizes the duty of vigilance and self-criticism at every point in philosophizing.

Page 35: Jaspers is accused of 'love of the exceptional', whereas his aim throughout is to do justice both to the exception and to the universal. He would say that we must learn from the exceptional individual, though we are not called upon to be such ourselves. Bobbio has treated one small section of Jaspers's philosophy as though it were the key to the whole.

Page 50: 'The attitude he adopts towards the problem of the relationship between my ego and my neighbour's ego smacks of an introversive and individualistic conception of ethics in which intercourse between men is a contact of souls which seek and find one another outside society and hence outside history, not an interweaving of social actions.' In the first place, Jaspers is concerned with communication, not between egos, but between existences, genuine persons. Secondly, he definitely asserts that communication takes place within history and the given social institutions, using these to fill relationships within them with a richer content, as reason employs the categories of understanding in order to transcend them.

Helmut Kuhn in *Encounter with Nothingness* (1951), 153f., actually speaks of Jaspers as bidding us *will* catastrophe and describing shipwreck as a 'happy calamity'. I do not recall a single line that admits of being thus understood.

III

Sein und Zeit. One could not expect a survey of history from Sartre, since he has no interest in the past and no understanding of tradition. It is doubtful where there is such a thing as history, as opposed to the histories of various peoples and civilizations, unless there is some initial belief in the unity of the human race. Such unity is incapable of proof, and there are times when the cleavages between different sections of the human race and different periods of history are so serious that it is not easy to retain one's faith. The Biblical myth of Adam as the parent of mankind has made it possible for Western man to survey the human enterprise, fragmentary as our knowledge of it is, as a total process, so that it is possible to ask after its meaning.[1]

When we compare the interpretation of history offered by Jaspers with those associated with the names of Spengler and Toynbee, we are struck by the fact that freedom plays a much larger part with him than it does with them. While Toynbee does not share the fatalistic approach of Spengler, he traces a recurrent pattern in the rise, decline, and fall of civilizations, so that, while he makes no attempt to forecast the future, he can define the issues that must be decided in it. The world today is at the cross-roads, but it is free to decide whether it will turn towards catastrophe or towards renewal. Jaspers, as might be expected, is yet more insistent on freedom and much less inclined to generalize. He is perhaps unfair to Toynbee in failing to recognize the fundamental difference at this point between him and Spengler. But he is surely right when he denies

---

[1] *Vom Ursprung und Ziel der Geschichte* (1949).

that there is a standpoint outside history that we can occupy while we survey it. There is no such standpoint, we are participants in history, not mere spectators of it. Nor is history for him the sum of past events as they have been recorded. In fact history is still open, since the future has yet to be made, and our present choices give a new turn even to the past, so that what it means is in part dependent on what we do now. No view of history can be separated finally from the total attitude to life of the one who attempts it. The scale of values by which he operates here will largely determine what he sees there.[1] In other words, a philosophy of history, like every other type of philosophy, is rooted in a personal faith.

Jaspers makes no attempt to conceal that it is a conviction of this order that leads him to find the Axis of history, as he calls it, the crucial period, in the one that runs from 800 to 200 B.C. It was confined, of course, to three points on the earth's surface, to Egypt-Mesopotamia, India, and China. The spiritual leaders of all subsequent history emerged in it, Confucius and Lao Tse, the writers of the Upanishads and Buddha, Zoroaster and the prophets of Israel, Socrates and the Greek philosophers and tragedians. It was the birth-hour of man as a spiritual being. He began to sound the depths and to aspire to the heights. His eye was turned inwards upon the soul and outwards upon ultimate

[1] So recently E. H. Carr: *The New Society* (1951), 18: 'His (the historian's) aims and purposes will ultimately be derived from values which have their source outside history; for without these history itself must become meaningless—a mere succession of action for the sake of action, and change for the sake of change.'

reality. He passed from the world of myth to the world of reason and conscience. He achieved independence but knew that he was not his own master. It was at this period that the questions were first asked that since then have been raised afresh in each generation, that the moral insights were won—or should we say granted?—with which we cannot dispense at this day.

To be sure, history did not begin with the Axis. The human race was already old. The great civilizations of Egypt and Babylon, India and China, were securely established. They provided the material basis for the spiritual advance it achieved. How and why it arose out of them we do not know; we must consent to mystery. And behind these ancient civilizations stretches the long prehistoric period during which man was in the making and of which so little has survived to us. For history only begins with tradition, whose office it is to make the past available in the present. Again, there are many peoples who remain to this day untouched by the high civilizations and by the spiritual achievements of the Axis period. For here again is a mystery, that the movements to which we owe so much were not given to all. To this day a people enters into history as we understand it just at the point at which it takes over this social and spiritual heritage, whether in its Eastern form or its Western.

We who live in Europe today are children of a second and equally formative period, the one that began with the Renaissance and ran through Rationalism, the French Revolution, the Industrial Revolution and so on to where we now stand. The master agency

here is the rise of modern science, and once again we
note with awe that this was not granted to all mankind
—it is a privilege of the West. If we ask how it was
that it arose there and nowhere else, our only answer
will consist in pointing out certain features in Western
civilization that were favourable. The questioning
spirit of Greece and the Christian doctrine of creation
are not the least important among these.[1] We may mention also the diversity among the European peoples,
with the conflicts that ensued and made stagnation
impossible, as also the clash of creed upon creed and
the tension between Church and State. But we must
allow also for the appearance of exceptional individuals
who were more than the product of their time, the
pioneers who discovered new possibilities and so made
them available for all.

Science develops the type of mind that combines
passion for the minutest detail with the urge towards a
comprehensive whole of knowledge, scepticism with
openness to new facts. But it has brought forth something else, technology, mass-civilization, and the
machine, with all their effects, sometimes beneficial and
sometimes terrifying. Technology is the manipulation
of the material environment in the interest of human
life, and its peculiar triumph was the Industrial Revolution, a product of science, the spirit of invention, and
the large-scale organization of labour. The technical
civilization of the West today overspreads the whole
earth, bringing within its influence peoples untouched
by the Axis and owing nothing to the ancient civiliza-

[1] Cf. A. N. Whitehead: *Science and the Modern World*, 15ff.

tions that preceded it. So momentous are the effects of the Renaissance and what followed on it that we might be tempted to speak of it as a second Axis. But this we may not do. The new period does not enlarge man's spiritual vision as the old one did. It puts him in mortal peril, for technology threatens to subdue even the soul of man to itself.

Standing as we do in the midst of this modern period, two results become clear to us. The first is that we live for the first time in one world. The remotest peoples are having the appurtenances of Western civilization forced upon them. A world unfolds before us for which European history is but a provincial affair, democracy a rare and rather unsuccessful experiment in political techniques, and Christianity a comparatively recent arrival among religions. We of the West have not yet realized that we must play a much more modest part henceforth. What lies beyond the Atlantic in one direction and beyond the Urals in another will decide our fate. India and China must be accepted as equal partners at first, perhaps as superior before long. The values we have dismissed as aberrations from our standards now claim to be ranked as of the same right as our own. The war of 1914-18 was no world war, it was a mere European quarrel; only now do we know what global war is like.

The second result is that the spiritual life is in grave danger, for man himself is in process of becoming mechanized. Today the mass is the deciding factor, in taste as in politics. Can we educate the individual, embedded from birth in the mass, to conscience and responsibility, to truth in the inward parts? If not, what will our fate be? Modern man has learned cynicism, he questions everything that he hears; what opposes him he dismisses as ideology, but at the same time he is capable of almost limitless self-deception. We have forgotten such things as simplicity and fellowship and have handed life over to organization. We dwell amid negations, being anti-this and anti-that. When distress of soul stirs us, we roll off our guilt upon any scapegoat that is handy. We are victims of unbelief and nihilism. Yet these are not our fate. If we understand them we should be able to bring them under control. Our one hope of overcoming the monsters that threaten us is to confront them fearlessly and to take the measure of their power to injure us.

Man today seeks after freedom, prizing it under both its forms, as the liberation of the innermost self and as the rule of law in organized society. But freedom has to be won and maintained in face of the three great tendencies of the time; we must be able to make these our servants or they will show themselves masters. The first tendency is *Socialism*. Our mass-society, particularly as it has been affected by two world wars, cries out for large-scale organization and economic planning. We are therefore tempted to push this too far, to make it total. But that is incompatible with freedom. Planning must be kept within definite limits and confined to goods of a lower order. Jaspers would wish, for example, to retain the free market. We must not worship applied science as though it can solve all problems. For man in the last resort lives by much that can only be given to him and can never be organized and administered.

The second tendency is towards *world unity*. Such unity is inevitable. Wars there may be in the future, but they will be in the nature of civil wars, rending a unity that must be composed again thereafter. The question that remains is whether unity will take the form of world empire or world order. Either one of the two great Powers that alone remain will beat down all opposition and coerce us into a new *Pax Romana*, or we shall learn to live in mutual understanding. To achieve the latter, some form of federation will be the step necessary. There will have to be a surrender of sovereignty, at least to the extent of bringing into being a centre of power that will permit to member-states the exercise of certain functions, while reserving the rest to itself. Perhaps Russia or the United States will begin such a federation with the states attached to it, and this will grow until it takes in the whole world. We are no longer asked whether we will unite, but only under what form we will do so.

There is, however, a third need, the greatest of all. It is for a *faith* that will counter the nihilism and unbelief already spoken of. We recognize some of the features of our own time in the spectacle of ancient Rome in its decay. What is lacking from the contemporary picture is anything so virile and so promising as early Christianity was. Clearly, the faith that is to hearten and unite us can be no manufactured product. We do not need, on the other hand, any new revelation, but only the rebirth of the religion of the Bible in a form appropriate to our time and its needs. It will be faith in God, bringing to men the conviction that they are not alone in face of circumstance nor at the mercy of their own impulses, but that there is a Power that supports their honest endeavours and gives lasting significance thereto. It will be faith in man, so that even an age haunted by the nightmare horrors of Buchenwald will be capable of toleration and the recognition of another as of equal worth with oneself. It will be faith in the possibilities of the future, so that ideals will be given to us that will inspire and direct our action in this stubborn yet inviting world.

So all turns in the end upon the responsibility of the individual. Only he who sees that this is so today will interpret history as Jaspers does, for the crux of that interpretation is the recognition of the hour in the past at which the individual awoke to his responsibility as the axis on which all history turns. There are no forces of good that bear us forward to our salvation while we remain passive. But if our problems can be solved only by action, we must not forget that action can only be fruitful in the measure in which it is guided by thought. And for both thought and action there is a further guide in faith, faith that man was made in the image of God, that he is one amid all his divisions, and that it is not without a purpose that he is on the earth.

We may sum up briefly. History is not a process intended to reach some particular state of things as its goal. Its meaning is here and now, in the content that can enter into each moment as it is lived in freedom, with God and with one's fellows; therefore its meaning

is in the future also and was in the past, since the same
meeting with God will be and was possible at all times.
It is the sphere in which man reveals himself in his
potentialities for good and evil, the sphere also in
which God reveals himself in and through our response
to him. The meaning of history is to be found if we
look, not forward to some goal to which the present is
but as means to an end, but within and at the same
time above.[1]

(c)

Again and again in this discussion there has been
occasion to use the word 'faith'. Never perhaps has an
academic philosopher laid such stress on faith as
Jaspers does. But the faith of which he speaks is philosophical rather than religious. The main difference
between the two is that the one is individual, without
authority and without security, while the other is the
bond of common life within a church and rests upon a
revelation that gives assurance. The philosopher must
win his faith by personal wrestling with the great problems of life, and, however precious his faith may be to
him, it cannot be exempted from the critical processes of
reason. He must feel his way forward, live by tentative
solutions, and acknowledge always that the truth he has
grasped is but a broken fragment of the whole. Above
all, he must live in independence and may not bind
himself to any person or institution in the world. No

[1] The greater part of this section reproduces, with slight changes, the
article on 'The Axis of History' in the *Contemporary Review* for April, 1950
(with permission).

man can be the incarnation of God, no book or church can be infallible, no revelation is possible save in and through the limitations of some historical situation. The philosopher is therefore denied the guarantees that are given to the believer; yet he does not envy him these, for he is convinced that in taking his own way he does not walk in arrogance but under God's guidance.

This faith belongs to existence, that is, it is an attitude of the self to what transcends it and the world, an attitude that by its very nature seeks communication. Yet, as we have seen, all communication has its price; it requires that we throw what claims our whole being into the form of propositions that can be defended. We must speak of the world that transcends all knowledge of objects as though it were another object, since otherwise we should be unable to speak of it at all. It is possible therefore to throw the content of philosophical faith into the form of statements, though it must be borne in mind always that these are not true *qua* statements, but only as expressions of a total attitude of the self. All metaphysical statements are of this order, Jaspers would say. We have to use the categories of the understanding to express that which arises at the point where all our categories break down. We have to use the objects in this world as signs and symbols of the Transcendent. Their truth does not lie in what they express literally but in that to which they point, and what they yield is not an addition to our knowledge but a transformation of our very selves.

This opens up the possibility of a new kind of

natural theology. It will not be a knowledge of God that is reached by unaided human reasoning, but one that is attested by the conscience and won in the encounter with life's hazards. Especially at the limit-situations of life, such as pain, conflict, guilt, death, and the sheer facticity, the givenness of our being-here, we are awakened to that which can never be an object of knowledge but which offers itself to be received and apprehended by our whole selves. It might be better to call it 'elemental religion'. Of course, for Jaspers the faith he describes does not derive its value from any function as a schoolmaster to lead men to Christ: whether it is or is not supplemented and completed by revealed truth is not for him, as a philosopher, to say. But he would certainly—and surely with right—question the possibility of any revelation that does not need to be personally accepted and assimilated.

He would reject the exclusive claim of the Biblical revelation. God was known to Plato and Aristotle and not to the Hebrew prophets alone. He speaks of the God of the Greek thinkers as 'originating in thought'. I should myself prefer to say that such knowledge of God as they had was in fact existential in origin and that their arguments about God were, as all such arguments indeed are, only so many symbols of a truth reached by a quite different path. Jaspers considers the claim of philosophy to prove or disprove God's existence and agrees with Kant in rejecting this. For 'a proved God would be no God but merely a thing in the world'.[1] His own faith and what I have called

1 *Way to Wisdom*, 42.

his natural theology are not purely philosophical, however; they are avowedly deeply indebted to the Bible, especially to the prophets. We have evidence that he devoted much time to the study of Jeremiah during his enforced retirement under the National Socialist régime, and he makes moving use of a passage from him at the close of his discussion of Germany's war-guilt.[1] He sometimes speaks of the Bible as revelation and sometimes refuses to it this character. Probably this means that he does not accept it as inspired in the traditional sense, but reads it as the record of how men met God at the limit-situations of their life and prevailed through him. They were, of course, men of another age, while we must live in our own. We may therefore only take over from the Bible what convinces our reason and conscience, so that we live faithfully in our situation as the heroes of old did in theirs. The result of all this is that the philosophical faith for which Jaspers stands is the ethical monotheism of the great prophets, especially Jeremiah and Second Isaiah. It has less in common with the New Testament, as we shall see in the next section.

The time has now come to consider two statements of this faith that Jaspers puts forward in his *Way to Wisdom*, twelve radio talks from Basel. It is most convenient to take the shorter of these as a commentary on the first article in the longer, for such indeed it is.

(a) *God is*. By this is not meant that there is a supreme object God whose existence can be inferred from the world. All arguments for God give us what is not God

---

[1] *Die Schuldfrage* (1946), 96.

in so far as they are conclusive. They only lead us to God when we find that they break down and leave us in the presence of mystery. God is not the First Cause, he is the point at which the causal concept becomes fantastically inapplicable and we find ourselves asking the question to which there is no answer: Why is there anything at all and not rather nothing? 'God is not an object of knowledge, of compelling evidence. He cannot be experienced by the senses. He is invisible, he cannot be seen but only believed in.'[1] God is not to be demonstrated, he is to be met with. Where do we meet him? In the exercise of our freedom. God, that is, is not the one who relieves us of the exercise of freedom and responsibility, but the one who makes this possible for us. It is as I live out of my freedom, not surrendering to my environment or living at second-hand by the opinion of others, but acting out of my freedom, that I realize that I am not self-caused, I have been given to myself. Then it is I meet with God.

If we are to say more of God, we can do it best in the language of the Bible.

(i) *Thou shalt not make unto thee any graven image or likeness*. God is absolute and everything in this world is relative. We may not therefore identify him with it, drag him down to its level. All our language concerning God is symbolic, true only when taken as metaphor and image, false once it is taken as adequate to his splendour. Idolatry is not confined to the worship of things that are taken for a likeness of God; it is present when we cease to recognize the abyss that separates

---

[1] *Ibid.*, 44.

even our highest conception of God from God himself. True, we must use human language to express him, since it is the only medium at our disposal; yet the silence that transcends all speech, worship in awe and wonder, the peace that passeth understanding— these apprehend him where words break down.

(ii) *Thou shalt have no other gods before me.* There is only one God. Monotheism is not an abstract proposition, it is the grounding of one's whole self upon a single commanding allegiance, and that to nothing less than God. 'Concentration on the One gives to the decision of existence its real foundation.'[1]

(iii) *Thy will be done.* God is beyond our human reckoning, yet not in the sense that he flouts our human standards. His ways with us are inscrutable, yet we have faith that they are just. Like Job, we appeal from the God who lays waste our life and robs us of happiness to the God whom we know in our hearts; though he slay us, yet we will trust in him. Therefore we accept the harsh discipline of life as from the same hand that bestows upon us so much good; we go forward in hope and courage even where we cannot understand. 'He knoweth the way that I take; when he hath tried me, I shall come forth as gold.'

(*b*) *There is an unconditional imperative.* While everything here below is relative, that does not mean that our life is robbed of any contact with what is absolute. Rather does eternity enter time in the fateful 'moment' of which Kierkegaard spoke. Granted that most of our life is determined for us rather than by us, that we act

[1] *Ibid.*, 49.

out of custom and habit rather than from our innermost selves, do there not come to us, if only twice or thrice in the course of a lifetime, occasions in which we are conscious that all is at stake, that to choose wrongly is to lose our very selves? A choice made at such a time is not one decision alongside otherwise; we do not so much will it as will out of it; it is rather constitutive of our selfhood than an expression of it. We may or may not be able to justify what we do at such a time; a call is addressed to us from the Transcendent and we can but obey. At such an hour we live the eternal life in the midst of time, for past, present, and future are not dimensions in which we live; we are their master and fuse them into the unity of a single creative action.

(c) *Man is finite and imperfectible.* Great as man is, his glory lies beyond himself. 'Man is a being who exists in relation to God. . . . We men are never adequate to ourselves. We press beyond, and we ourselves grow with the depth of our consciousness of God, through which at the same time we apprehend our insignificance.'[1] To be sure, this relation to God is not accessible to knowledge, no text-book of anthropology mentions it, it escapes the psychologist's notice; only in the acceptance of our freedom and responsibility are we aware of it. Then we know ourselves to be frail and mortal, with limited knowledge and wisdom, never satisfied with ourselves. There is a hunger in us no material progress can satisfy, a sickness no social planning can cure; man can never be his own saviour.

(d) *Man can live in God's guidance.* For him who says

---

[1] *Ibid.*, 64f.

126

to God: 'Thy will be done', knowledge of that will will not be lacking. True, it will never take the form of ready-made solutions to our problems, there is no human authority that speaks with the voice of God; we must find our way forward at the risk of error and catastrophe. For God communicates with us and guides only by our freedom; our strength and wisdom therefore are rooted in humility before him.

(e) *The reality of the world subsists ephemerally between God and existence.* The traditional argument for God as First Cause is logically invalid, as Kant showed. But it is capable of an existential translation; the world in which I know myself to be set is not self-sufficient, it is dependent even as I am. Scientific knowledge is neither total nor final, it is an excerpt from a larger whole. Yet the world can mediate to us God and our true selves. We find God, sometimes as we rise above it and sometimes again as we enter into it to hallow it. For God speaks to us by the world yet never gives himself wholly to us in it; the revelation of God is also his reticence; all things here below are signs and symbols of him, but none of them is to be identified with him.

None of these principles is capable of demonstration; they are reached by faith in open and responsible dealing with life and in communication, equally open and responsible, with our partners in life. They are true only while they are expressions of personal commitment, and as such they have their own certainty.

'The God of faith is the distant God, the hidden God, the indemonstrable God.'

'Hence I must recognize not only that I do not know

127

God but even that I do not know whether I believe.
Faith is no possession. It confers no secure knowledge,
but it gives certainty in the practice of life.

'Thus the believer lives in the enduring ambiguity
of the objective, in enduring willingness to hear. He
listens patiently and yet he is unswerving in his resolve.
In the cloak of weakness he is strong, he is open,
though in his real life he is resolute.'[1]

(d)

The faith that inspires the reading of history just
outlined has, as we saw, been described by Jaspers as
philosophical rather than religious. It might be more
accurate to describe it as theistic and even Biblical, but
not specifically Christian. He recognizes that the influence of Christianity is still all-pervading in the
Western world, albeit in secularized forms. In particular, philosophy cannot but concern itself with the
problems it has raised and inquire whether the insights
it has communicated to us are not valid even where its
dogmas are no longer acceptable. His own attitude to
Christianity can never therefore be a negative one; he
must be 'a heretic within the Church, essentially a
Protestant'.[2] He draws on the Biblical religion, while
rejecting the version of that religion current in the
churches today.

It would be misleading to attempt in any way to slur

[1] *Ibid.*, 50 f.
[2] Quoted in Erich Frank: 'Die Philosophie von Jaspers', *Theologische Rundschau*, Neue Folge (1933), 318.

over his quarrel, as a philosopher, with organized religion. He is prepared to defend it against its critics on many counts, but only on the understanding that he is allowed to pass his own adverse judgment where he feels this to be called for. The gravamen of his charge against it is its intolerance, the pride with which it claims possession of an absolute truth and brands as sinners those who hesitate to accept this.

In various works from his *Philosophie* onwards, Jaspers has sought to define his attitude to Christianity and its claims. The most guarded and detailed of all such attempts is to be found in a section of his massive work on philosophical logic,[1] and I shall follow this mainly in the rest of the present section.

At the outset, a distinction is established between the conflict of religion and philosophy and that between Catholicity and reason. In the former case, we have polarities between which there will always be tension, but each of which can and should recognize the full rights of the other. In the second case, we are confronted by a sharp *Either-Or*, to choose one is to reject the other as erroneous. We have described earlier in this chapter what Jaspers understands by reason; we must now define what he means by Catholicity. The immediate reference is not to the Catholic Church as such but to a tendency that comes to its clearest expression in that communion. 'Catholicity arises where a configuration in the world, an event, the Word as Holy Scripture, a special cultus and all these

---

[1] *Von der Wahrheit* (1947), 832ff. See also *The Perennial Scope of Philosophy* (1949), 75ff.

together in the unity of a Church claim to have equal validity for all men.'[1] It is this claim to an objectivity and universality comparable to that of science in a region which, as Jaspers sees it, is penetrable only by a personal conviction that is at once historically conditioned and exposed to error, that is for him an offence against the philosophical reason. As we shall see, he does not reject authority as such, he is convinced that freedom is only possible as it is grounded in authority. But here, he would say, freedom has to contend against an authority that would destroy it were it established. We may follow him as he develops the argument step by step.

To begin with, he investigates more closely the nature of the two parties and their opposition.

(a) Catholicity stands for an objective, reason for a subjective, absolute. That is to say, Catholicity elevates a historical phenomenon to the rank of the unconditioned; reason lives by the unconditioned that lays hold upon me personally and wins my unreserved allegiance. Catholicity demands that all men come over to its point of view, that they become Christians, that all other religions lose themselves in Christianity eventually; reason bids each man live out of his own historical tradition, while freely recognizing the right of others to live out of their quite different traditions. The one breeds fanatics who demand submission, the other is tolerant and generous, ever eager to learn while faithful to its own heritage.

(b) For Catholicity the meaning of history is

[1] Op. cit., 866f.

summed up and given, ready made, in one section of history, an event in the past and an institution that takes its rise from this; there is therefore nothing more to learn. For reason, on the other hand, the meaning of history lies in the total process, which is as yet incomplete and handed over to our freedom. History is authoritative for it, but as a dynamic and not a static authority, one that accompanies us to guide our venture and not one that lays down in advance the lines within which we are to move. There are here two opposed conceptions of unity. Unity for Catholicity is an observable entity within the world; for reason it is beyond the world: all the unities we achieve are but partial and symbols of the unity to which we aspire, by faith in which we live, but which we can never hold in our hands.

(c) Catholicity offers a total knowledge from which solutions of problems and rules of conduct can be deduced; reason lives by the certitude that is won moment by moment in the face of doubt and uncertainty. The one creates systems, the other knows only a broken world in which each of us, at the risk of error, wins such assurance as is compatible with the human condition.[1]

(d) Catholicity seeks to guide humanity by means of a single fixed authority, arguing that since God is one

---

[1] It is worth remarking that here, as elsewhere in the analysis, Jaspers recognizes that Catholicity may take the form of a philosophical system. That is particularly the case with Hegel, who represents his own system as the goal and consummation of the whole philosophical effort down the centuries, a point beyond which progress is not possible, since an absolute conclusion has been reached.

he must disclose himself for us under this form; for reason God reveals himself in and through a variety of authorities, each of which is historically conditioned and to be appropriated by freedom. No one authority can claim to sit in judgment on the rest, and truth is to be found, not by submission, but by the exercise of our own insight and freedom. 'The truth that lies at the foundation of all truths comes to realization in communication between the various great historical authorities.'[1]

(e) The two opponents differ fundamentally in the methods they employ. Catholicity creates a grandiose system in which everything has its place, and which is now closed, so that nothing can be admitted from outside; reason is open always to the new, the challenging, and the strange, since there also truth is to be found. Catholicity allows the end to justify the means, it permits virtually everything if only allegiance is given to the system; reason is scrupulous, self-critical, and demands self-consistency. Catholicity has recourse to *Realpolitik*; reason only prevails by winning consent. Reason represents the will to open and unlimited communication, seeking to find common ground even with those who reject reason. And communication always employs the maieutic of Socrates, the indirect method of Kierkegaard; 'it gives impulse but not help'.[2]

It is clear from this last paragraph that the issue is no merely theoretical one. Catholicity is an attitude

---

[1] *Ibid.*, 842.
[2] *Ibid.*, 847.

that has the gravest possible consequences. Jaspers suggests that it is by no accident that the totalitarian régimes have grown up on the soil of a Christian civilization. Only men accustomed to think of themselves as in possession of the absolute truth would be capable of the political furies and fanaticisms that have brought Europe to such misery in our day. Intolerance, too, is reflected in the attitude of the theologian towards those who differ from him. So Jaspers can say:

'It is among the sorrows of my life spent in the search for truth, that discussion with theologians always dries up at crucial points; they fall silent, state an incomprehensible proposition, speak of something else, make some categoric statement, engage in amiable talk, without really taking cognizance of what one has said—and in the last analysis they are not really interested. For on the one hand they are certain of their truth, terrifyingly certain; and on the other hand, they do not regard it as worth while to bother about people like us, who strike them as merely stubborn. . . . No one who is in definitive possession of the truth can speak properly with someone else—he breaks off authentic communication in favour of the belief he holds.'[1]

In a contest of this kind, the brave man chooses to challenge the opponent where he is strongest. Jaspers does this. He confronts the Christian doctrine of the God-Man. That God should have become man, eternity time, at a definite point in the past, that he should be the pattern for all, the atoning sacrifice for

---

[1] *The Perennial Scope of Philosophy*, 77.

133

all, the spiritual nourishment of all by his flesh and blood—this is for philosophy *the* stone of stumbling and the rock of offence. And many theologians would agree, their confession runs *Credo quia absurdum*. For Kierkegaard the God-Man is the impossible become actual, the absurd, the absolute paradox that constrains men either to believe or to take offence.

'The possibility of offence, in the one form or the other, accompanies the God-Man every instant, a man's shadow does not accompany a man more inseparably than the possibility of offence accompanies the God-Man, for the God-Man is the object of faith. The God-Man (and by this, as has been said, Christianity does not understand that fantastic speculation about the unity of God and man, but an individual man who is God)—the God-Man exists only for faith; but the possibility of offence is just the repellent force by which faith comes into existence—if one does not choose instead to be offended.'[1]

Jaspers sees clearly that the only question worth asking about this is: Is it true? Did God actually come to earth as a Jewish carpenter nineteen centuries ago? If he did, then we must accept him as God. But there are certain tests that can be applied, and the result in each case is negative.

The first test is: 'By their fruits ye shall know them.' One can set side by side the great representatives of faith in the God-Man, Paul, Augustine, Luther, Calvin, and the great representatives of philosophical faith, Plato, Shakespeare, Kant, Goethe. What is the result?

[1] Kierkegaard: *Training in Christianity* (1941), 122.

134

'Not a distinction in the degree of love with which we regard these men, but a qualitative distinction, in so far as we shrink from them or find ourselves drawn to them in love.'[1]

Again, every philosophy that is more than superficial must allow the rights of the absurd and the paradoxical; in Jaspers's own metaphysics this can be a symbol of the Transcendent. But there is nothing in common between a paradox that leads us to the Godhead and a paradox that fetters us to dogma; the first releases freedom, the second destroys it. Finally, however we may be drawn in reverence to the figure of Jesus, there is that in him which repels. Kierkegaard's merit was that he saw this and clung to it against the world. He has shown us what the imitation of Christ finally means; it led him to self-torment, isolation from his fellows, intolerance, repudiation of marriage and the family, in short, to utter hatred of life itself. It is idle to protest that Kierkegaard does not represent the genuine Christian tradition, that this has entered into the life of the Western nations, inspiring their art and their social forms, that it has been a leaven for good in the world rather than flight from it. Jaspers would reply that in Christianity as it has developed through the centuries he can see only a gigantic compromise forced by the necessities of their situation upon those who had made the initial error of glorying in the absurd.

As symbols, no doubt, Christ and his Cross will always be potent. The philosopher will value them as the believer does, though he will interpret them in his

---

[1] *Von der Wahrheit*, 853.

own way. They will speak to him rather of the inadequacy of the human to the divine than of their identity in this one instance. But Catholicity as such he can only oppose. The choice between the two is the most fundamental one there is. 'For philosophizing the choice is one that decides about philosophizing itself, whether it is to take place or not.'[1] One cannot at the same time be ruled by an infallible authority and guided by freedom. One cannot both possess the truth and seek it. There are contradictions in our experience that can be resolved, but this is not one of them: we are presented with alternatives between which we must choose. The only limit reason can recognize is that which is set by its own nature; it cannot be tolerant of intolerance, it must therefore resist—though always with its own weapons—the claim of any institution, however venerable and useful, to have the whole truth and to require men to accept this from it without demur.

Hence each party to the dispute cannot but regard the other as dangerous and wholly in error. Even at this point, however, reason is capable of generosity to its antagonist. For it can recognize that Catholicity must and even ought to continue. It is perhaps indispensable to the spiritual life as far as the vast majority of men are concerned; they would faint beneath the burden of independent endeavour. Perhaps also reason can only come into full possession of itself as it has this foe always present to challenge it. The opposition is an irreconcilable one, and philosophy

[1] *Ibid.*, 858.

must be prepared to accept Catholicity as something with which it will always have to reckon.

Here we revert to the distinction drawn at the outset between the opposition authority *versus* freedom and that of Catholicity *versus* reason. Philosophy does not oppose authority as such but only this form it has assumed. For authority there will always be a place in human life. Such freedom as we may achieve is never more than partial, and so long as we are not yet capable of full independence we should welcome guidance. 'That word 'guidance' is the crux of the matter. Philosophy draws upon tradition, it knows itself immensely indebted, as a present activity, to great souls in the past; it follows such of these as command its allegiance, but it will be the slave of none. There are other traditions, too, those of family, nation, civilization, etc., without which we could not live. But all these are relative authorities, none is beyond criticism, to none do we tender blind submission. We live by them as we inwardly appropriate them.

Among such authorities, a high place must be given to the Bible. For Jaspers is convinced that the Bible, rightly understood, does not make the claim to absolute truth that Christianity makes for itself. Neither does it, at least in the Gospels, present Jesus as the God-Man: those words 'Why callest thou me good? there is none good save one, that is, God' must be taken to mean what they say. He who said them recognized God as other than himself, as one before whom he bowed in humility. The Bible is no closed system, it contains a dozen different types of religion, some of which we may accept while others we cannot but refuse. The God-Man and the Atonement can be removed and the vital message of the Bible still remains. It is a message of the living God and his will for men. Nothing perhaps is more needed today than a rediscovery of this.

(e)

One can hardly imagine a professional theologian taking seriously the contents of the previous section. He will be disposed to dismiss it as the last kick of a dying Liberal Protestantism that ought surely to have been dead and buried long ago. It is quite true that Jaspers appears to be sadly ill-informed on the New Testament and to be dominated still by a supposed opposition between Jesus and Paul. I do not think it is any longer possible to present the latter as the man who falsified the simple Galilean gospel and created out of reverence for a teacher the cult of the divine Christ. The essential Pauline positions seem to me to be rather taken over, with original and creative expansions of course, from the Primitive Church than directly produced by him. While I agree that the Jesus of the Synoptics is not the God-Man of the Nicene Creed, I am inclined to think that Mark already ascribes to him a metaphysical divinity. More important still, I am convinced that Jesus thought of himself as God's representative on earth, empowered with his authority, and of his death as in some sense an atonement for sin. In my judgment, therefore, the traditional, the liberal, and the neo-orthodox pictures of the relation between

138

Biblical religion and Christian theology are alike too simple and do not do justice to the evidence. Yet there is much in Jaspers's criticism to which the theologian would do well to give heed. The words 'He that is not against us is for us' are applicable here. The fact that 'he followeth not us' is no ground for condemnation. We who speak in the name of the God of the Bible are not so potent or persuasive that we can afford to bid another silence when he makes the same appeal in different language. There is sufficient suspicion of the professional theologian to lend peculiar authority to the man who calls us to God as a layman and a philosopher. We should be clear, too, that we are defending the Christian cause against these strictures and not merely our own. It is one of the besetting sins of the theologian that he does not distinguish clearly enough between God's truth and his own apprehension of it. Another is that he evades frank discussion by accusing the critic of unbelief. We may not ask for submission to ourselves but only to the God whom we serve so inadequately, and we should suspect any conception of Christianity that does not allow that men may turn from it in complete honesty.[1]

But there are certain answers that may legitimately be made from the Christian standpoint to Jaspers's strictures.

(a) The sharp distinction he draws between religious

[1] So, e.g., Emil Brunner's *The Scandal of Christianity* (1951) describes the Gospel as something the natural man is bound to take offence at and thereby places its author beyond criticism. This is dangerously like the sophistry of the psycho-analyst, who can dismiss every objection to his analysis as one more piece of evidence that it is correct!

and philosophical faith seems to me to be a reflection of his Continental environment. He knows of Christianity in the form of three great churches, Catholic, Lutheran, and Reformed, each with its claim to authority as against the other two and all with a long tradition of intolerance and even of persecution. The British and American scenes are quite different. There vigorous Christian bodies have maintained a witness to a more personal and less institutionalized form of Christianity. I suspect, to be sure, that much of the faith even in our 'independent' churches is of the dependent variety, acceptance of tradition. But does not the preacher tirelessly appeal to his hearers to pass beyond this stage to personal appropriation of the truth? Is it the Easter message that the problem of death has been solved once for all so that we need not distress ourselves about it, or that we conquer death as we, each in his turn, die with Christ and rise again with him? How many times have the words of Paul, 'last of all, he appeared to me also', been used to emphasize this! Faith is the moment in which the objective becomes subjective, what was true without me becomes true for me. Did not a Christian mystic say:

> The cross on Golgotha
> Can never save thy soul.
> The cross in thine own heart
> Alone can make thee whole?

Catholicity is one type of Christianity, but it is not by any means the only one.[1]

---

[1] In this paragraph and those that follow I have made use (with permission) of material contained in my article on 'Philosophy and the Bible in Karl

(*b*) In refusing to go beyond theism to the specifically Christian faith Jaspers seems to me untrue to his own best insights. God, he would say, communicates with men by his reticence rather than his revelation. Precisely because he cares so much for us, he abstains from any degree of interference with our freedom. He works always by placing responsibility on us; he keeps himself in the background so that we may discover truth by our own effort, he allows us to be exposed to hazard and tried almost to the limit of endurance, lest he should stunt our manhood in its growth by coming to our assistance too soon. He is the *Deus absconditus* for our sake.

Yet it is one of the chief merits of this philosophy that it lays such stress on communication and on love as a sharing of life to the uttermost. One of its masterwords is 'commitment'; we find ourselves as we bind ourselves to others and to concrete tasks in daily life. The individual must enter into the other's situation and give himself to him in it; we are made as we give ourselves away thus. Why then should all this be denied to God? Should we not rather think of God as one who is continually involved in the world, in the human happinesses and tragedies with which it is fraught, as one who is for ever giving himself? Does God simply wait for us in the limit-situations of death, pain, guilt, conflict, and so on, withholding himself till we have met their challenge? Does he not actually enter into these

Jaspers' in *Theology* for March, 1952. For a full discussion from the standpoint of neo-orthodoxy the reader is referred to J. Sperna Weiland: *Philosophy of Existence and Christianity* (1951).

situations and meet us in them? If so, there is no reason
why the *Deus absconditus* should exclude the *Deus
revelatus*. God reserves himself sometimes as a prize for
which we struggle, but he also offers himself as a gift
to be received. The idea of grace is not unknown to
Jaspers; life itself is gift and grace, he would say.
Why not then allow that God may act on our be-
half, that there may be a real entry into history on his
part?

(*c*) While, however, I would be prepared to maintain that this type of existentialism not merely allows
but even requires that the possibility of a divine self-
giving to the uttermost be left open, I would concede
to Jaspers that it is not consistent with the acceptance
of the God-Man of Christian dogma. The evidence
available in the Gospels seems to me to put beyond
doubt that Jesus thought of himself as a man dependent on God. The witness of John is if anything more
definite on this point than that of the Synoptists. In any
case, the language of pre-existence, a divine descent to
earth, and a return to the Father must be taken symbol-
ically and not literally. The unity of God and man can
only be an ethical and personal unity, the accord between two wills. The God-Man of Christian theology
symbolizes not some general unity of the divine and
human as in Hegel's philosophy—Kierkegaard was
surely right on that point—but the total dedication in
Jesus of a human will to the divine purpose of love,
the divine act of self-giving in his human self-giving in
Galilee and on the Cross. So understood, it is possible
to see in Jesus God coming personally to us, yet with-

out identifying the two or conferring absolute value on
a life lived within historical limitations.[1]

(d) The message 'God was in Christ' therefore remains. The human life of Jesus was the beginning of
that deed of God for our salvation that continues to
this day in his presence with us as the Lord who con-
quered death and is alive for evermore. What claim do
we make for him? Not, I would say, an exclusive one,
as though all God's truth were in him. By the very fact
that he was a historical individual certain possibilities
were excluded; he was man and not woman, Jew and
not Greek, and so on. All the same, it may be doubted
whether any other figure can be compared with him in
the appeal he makes to races with different traditions
and values. He possesses a capacity to speak afresh to
each generation. That, however, is not the important
point. The claim of Christian faith for its Lord is that
he is of decisive significance for all men at all times. By
which we mean that when they are brought face to
face with him their attitude to him decides whether
they will enter into God's purpose for the world or
stand apart from it. And by that is not meant that they
are saved or lost according as they do or do not join
the Christian Church. A man's decision concerning
Christ is known to God only and is not to be equated
with his relation to any creed or institution. The
Christian, we may say, does not claim that Christ has a
monopoly of truth, but that all truth is seen most
adequately in his light. That is not some extra claim he
makes for Christ, it is why he is a Christian.

[1] See further on this my *Divine and Human* (1952), 55ff.

(e) I think one does more than make a debating-point when one directs the attention of those who urge that each man should live by his own tradition to the fact that we ourselves are only Christians today because our fathers did not do that. I fully agree that it is our duty to find and serve God within our historical situation and therefore in accordance with our tradition. But the position everywhere today is that traditions are being broken, all situations have become fluid. We of the West can no longer shut ourselves off from the spirituality of the East, and *vice versa*. It is greatly to be regretted when, let us say, an African becomes a Christian at the price of being uprooted and turned into a poor specimen of Western individualism, or when a Chinese Christian is insensitive to the values of the Confucian tradition. But missionaries are increasingly aware of these dangers and on their guard against them. That it is possible for an Indian or an African or a Chinese to live out of his own tradition and at the same time to be personally loyal to Christ has been proved again and again. The obligation to abide by the truth we have requires always to be supplemented by the obligation to seek the fullest possible truth.

(f) So we come finally to the all-important question of the relation between Christianity and other religions. I would begin by accepting the distinction between the absolute and the universally valid. The former is that which grips my whole being, so that I yield it unreserved allegiance. But this will always be historically conditioned, since it will be my truth, appropriate to my particular situation. Paradoxically, it will be absolute by being perfectly relative, or, if you prefer, perfectly adequate. The universally valid, on the other hand, is that which is true for all men under all conditions. As such, it will be abstract and impersonal like the laws of logic or the established conclusions of science. It will be relative also, though in a different way, since it can be apprehended only as one takes up a special standpoint, when one assumes the role of a spectator instead of an actor. In neither case, therefore, have we a truth on which an exclusive claim can be based. There is my neighbour's truth beside my own, as there are standpoints other than that of the scientific consciousness.

Now it is quite true that the absolute of religious conviction is a subjective absolute. In less technical language, it is personal and implicates the whole self in a manner that admits of no reserve. What I apprehend at such a moment fills my whole horizon, it enters me and remakes me, so that I am only in virtue of it. For the delivering instant my faith and my being coincide. The truth that saves me is the truth that speaks to *me*, to an Englishman of a certain age, social position, education, temperament, and life-history. But if it is to *save* me it must pierce through all this to what I am before God; it must deal with the universal human need implicit in my particular need. That is to say, it is true for me only as it is at the same time true for all men. It is universally valid, if you care to use that expression, but not as a scientific proposition is, because it is detached from all personal considerations. It is universally valid because it is so utterly personal, something for the soul in its need, yearning, and self-abandonment upon God.

How can we apply this to our special problem? The object of devotion is in the nature of the case incomparable—that is, it is in a class by itself and does not admit of being compared with others. He who truly loves his wife does not compare her with other women; the fact that he is beginning to do so is a sign that his love for her is in danger. This is even more the case with religious faith. To be sure, one who contemplates a change in his religion may compare, let us say, Christ and Buddha. But as long as he does so, he is neither a Christian nor a Buddhist; he is student and observer of two religious types. He only becomes a Christian or a Buddhist when he brings the process to an end, deciding to admit one of the two claimants to the throne of his being and thereby to exclude the other. The moment we undertake a comparison between our own religion and another we have changed what we are dealing with. Our religion is only such as it holds us, and it undergoes a change into something quite different when we hold it, as it were, at arm's length to be examined dispassionately. Or, to put the same thing in other words, we can compare our religion with another because our religion is not itself the object to which we give devotion but the particular and historically conditioned form under which we apprehend this. As such, it is relative, one instance out of a class of religions.

We have therefore to distinguish between two planes, the plane of devotion, on which a single allegiance shuts out all else for the time being, and the plane of comparison, on which two or more institutions, doctrines, and forms of worship are placed side by side. On this second plane there are several possible judgments, but only two need be considered here. The first is that one's own religion is exclusive and has a monopoly of truth, the second that it is one truth among a variety of available truths. Each of these judgments is in part true and in part false. The first is true in so far as it gives expression to the absolute commitment of faith, false in so far as it removes this conviction from the plane to which it belongs and projects it on the other, where it becomes perverted. The second judgment is true in so far as it expresses the humble acknowledgment that my truth is always human and imperfect, never to be identified with God's truth, false because it fails to do justice to the absolute commitment without which there would not have been such a thing as my truth.

Where then does the solution of our problem lie? It lies in the recognition that my truth is never God's truth as such, but at the best my limited apprehension of this, and sometimes quite certainly, alas, my misapprehension of it. In so far as it is of God, it is for all men and I am under an obligation to share it with them. In so far as it is of myself, I am under an obligation to place it alongside of what others have seen and to correct my insight by what I can learn from them. Truth, as Jaspers insists, is no man's private possession, it lies in communication. It is by openness to one another that we learn, yet how can we learn save as we give frank expression to our deepest convictions? It he supposes that we ask men to accept Christ on our authority or without inner conviction, as they might take over from us a knowledge of chemistry, he is seriously mistaken. We commend Christ to others in the sure confidence that he will authenticate himself to them and win them by inner conviction.

5. Through Mystery to Fidelity

THOSE who come to Marcel from the academic study of philosophy are likely to be disconcerted by what they find, particularly by the tentative manner in which he so often presents his conclusions. We turn over a few pages of his *Journal Métaphysique* and note here and there such remarks as: 'I must look more deeply into this' or 'I cannot see my way any further just now' or 'How is this to be reconciled with what I wrote last month? I do not know.' We are not taking over, whether for acceptance or for criticism, a system that someone else has worked out, we are being invited to listen in to a philosopher's day-to-day thinking. In his Gifford Lectures, Marcel invites us to explore with him a territory in which as yet he is only beginning to find his bearings. Sometimes he wanders from the track and must make his way back to it at the first opportunity. But the value of the expedition lies rather in the adventure and the quest than in the goal reached. 'Between a philosophical investigation and its final outcome, there exists a link which cannot be broken without the summing up itself immediately losing all reality.'[1]

[1] *The Mystery of Being* (1950), I, 5.

149

Through Mystery to Fidelity

Do we say that this is literature and not philosophy? Let us remember that one of the greatest of all philosophers adopted a not dissimilar method. In reading Plato's dialogues, can we always be sure with which of the speakers he identifies himself? Is that what is important in his eyes? Is not the dialogue-form meant rather as an invitation to us to take part in the inquiry by identifying ourselves with each of the participants in turn and so to reach a conclusion of our own? For Plato also, the conclusion is of no value apart from the process by which it has been attained. With Marcel as with Plato philosophy has grown out of life. Hence there is a personal and self-revealing quality about his writing such as one finds in Kierkegaard rather than in Jaspers, with whom otherwise he has so much in common.[1]

The comparison between Kierkegaard and Marcel may be carried a stage further. In each case, the creation of *dramatis personae* is the means chosen to explicate and communicate what is in the philosopher's mind. But there is in Marcel nothing at all corresponding to the elaborate cult of anonymity and the exploitation of his own private life that are so characteristic of Kierkegaard—and so questionable in him. The theatre provides a much simpler technique. Again, whereas every character delineated by Kierkegaard embodies some aspect of himself, either as what he is or what he might become, Marcel's are so effective because their life is

[1] I am quite unable to understand how Marjorie Grene can say of Marcel that 'something about the tone of his writing does not ring true' or that 'this is not genuine philosophizing but a two-faced, ambiguous, and not very clever imitation of it'. *Dreadful Freedom*, 130, 132.

wholly their own. It is just this independence that enables them to express him so well. For they are in no sense mouthpieces for his ideas, nor are they artificial types that he manipulates in the interest of some foregone conclusion. They are objective and seem to work out their own problems rather than any he has set them. Hence the deliberately inconclusive character of some of his dramas, noticeably *Le Chemin de Crête*. Was Ariadne a subtle schemer or a soul lifted above all normal jealousies? We are not told. The play makes us conscious of the mystery at the heart of each human personality. Can we judge the other? Do we even really know ourselves?

(a)

It will be clear from all this that there is a close connection between Marcel's own experience and the course his philosophy has taken. As the work reveals the man, so the man needs to be known to understand the work. He is himself well aware of this and has put us in his debt by the short autobiography in which he shows something of his development to date. He was an only child who lost his mother in early years, but he has retained till the present time a consciousness of her as in some mysterious fashion still present with him. His aunt and stepmother, who brought him up, held a creed remarkably like the atheist humanism of Camus.

'In the essentially uninhabitable world in which an incomprehensible play of circumstances had caused us to be born, there was only one resource: to forget oneself, to strive to lighten the burden of one's fellow-sufferers, and to submit to the most severe self-discipline, for outside this there was nothing but licence.'[1]

'From my earliest years,' he writes, 'I was haunted by the theatre, which attracted me less as a spectacle than as a privileged form of expression.' He was no doubt influenced in this by his father's passion for the theatre, but even more because it provided an escape from his lonely life. 'I have always thought that the imaginary characters with whom I held silent conversation replaced for me the brothers and sisters whom I so cruelly missed in real life.'[2]

His home training was meant in kindness but was felt by the lad as unduly severe. The highest of standards were set before him, he was closely supervised, and every detail of his work had a preposterous importance set upon it. He 'was racked by a kind of tension which at times reached an almost intolerable degree'.[3] It is not surprising, therefore, that in his dramas he so constantly warns against any imposition of oneself upon the life of another.

His environment as a child was one of agnosticism and moral strenuousness. Quite early in his philosophical studies, however, he became intrigued by the phenomena of religious faith. With his passion for the concrete, he was forced to admit that the philosopher

[1] *Philosophy of Existence* (1948), 81.
[2] *Ibid.*, 78.
[3] *Ibid.*, 82.

of today cannot escape the influence of Christianity; the language he uses and the society in which he lives are impregnated with Christian ideas. In his *Journal Metaphysique* he began therefore by assuming the Christian standpoint for the purposes of his study and inquiring how it could be justified. In the end this investigation led him to a personal decision, and on March 23, 1929, he was admitted into the Catholic Church by baptism. It would be grossly mistaken, however, to dismiss his philosophy as so much Catholic apologetic. Marcel moves rather at the level of what Jaspers would call philosophical faith. He is concerned with an elemental attitude to life that might be classed either as religious or as philosophical, and that may be found sometimes better exemplified in the agnostic than in the believer.

Another personal experience that deserves to be singled out for notice belonged to the First World War. Marcel was unfit for military service but undertook duties with the Red Cross. He was put in charge of an office that dealt with cases of men reported missing. His duty was to obtain what information was available and to break the news—usually the news that death should be presumed—to the relatives. He found that his work fell into two distinct and even opposed parts. On the one hand, he kept an elaborate card-index, for which each missing man was merely one more item to be catalogued. On the other, he had poignant and exacting interviews in which the same person became an individual loved and treasured, part of the very life of another. That stamped upon his mind the

all-important distinction between a problem and a
mystery. To this we now turn.

(*b*)

A problem is something 'out there' to which a detached attitude can be taken up; it is a question that has
been set to us by circumstances and to which we may
hope to find an answer. We have at our disposal a
technique that has been brought to perfection by multi-
tudes who have used it and has brilliant successes to its
credit. The technique is that of analysis. We break up
the problem into its component parts so that we may
handle it the more easily, we find some means of
assimilating it to what we already know, of bringing it
under familiar categories. We feel that we have suc-
ceeded when we have shown that it is not in fact the
novel and challenging thing we had thought it to be,
that it is 'really' something already known to us under
a different guise. Reduction follows on analysis. The
phenomenon from which we set out now becomes
'natural', it falls into its place, it is what might have
been expected, and so on. We have thus solved our
problem and in so doing have disposed of it, we can
go on to the next, for this particular one need not
trouble us again. And anyone who confronts the same
problem in the future will have no need to wrestle with
it as we have done, for he can take over our solution
ready-made.[1]

But not all problems are of so simple an order.

[1] In this section I have made use (with permission) of my article on
'Problem and Mystery' in *The Inquirer* for March 24, 1951.

Through Mystery to Fidelity

There are some that, as Marcel expresses it, trench upon their own data. We cannot detach them from ourselves and contemplate them. We are involved in them, they are part and parcel of our very selves. To break them up into their parts is to destroy them. We have not solved anything when we do this, we have substituted something quite different for what we are supposed to be dealing with. We are now in the realm of mystery, which lies beyond that of problems. Mystery can only be dealt with by some appropriate change of attitude on my part. The change from plural to singular is integral to the exposition, for mystery comes home to each one personally, though by doing so it establishes community between those who are thus drawn together. I cannot merely study and explain a mystery, I have to do something about it. And even then it will accompany me to life's end. But my commerce with it will not be in vain, for as I face the mystery with hope and courage, I shall grow into a richer self.

It is clear that the difference is that which Jaspers establishes between object knowledge and what transcends all such knowledge, so that it can be apprehended existentially or not at all. Mystery is not to be confused therefore with the mysterious in the usual sense of that term. When, for example, Robinson Crusoe found a footprint on the sands of his desert island, this was mysterious enough to call forth insecurity and fear on his part. But with further knowledge it ceased to be mysterious. It was a problem and he had solved it, it took its place among innumerable footprints in various parts of the world that were to be accounted for in substantially the same way. But we may imagine two parents standing by the cot in which their first child lies. One of them has received a scientific education while the other has not. But is that young life with its immense hidden potentialities any less mysterious to one than to the other? And when they join hands above the cot and renew their pledges of fidelity, are they not aware that they are within a mystery of personal relationship that no increase in knowledge will dissipate, that it will rather enhance?

One more point, and that an important one. Mystery in this sense is not to be confused with the unknown and the unknowable. It is not a problem we ought to be able to solve but cannot. It is not like the patch of ground that lies beyond my garden and that I may hope to bring under cultivation some day by purchasing it and extending the fence so as to take it in. It is like the air that can never be so manipulated, that requires to be approached in an altogether different way. Nor is mystery to be confused with those unreal problems we sometimes raise, the spurious mysteries that set us puzzling over questions that ought never to have been asked. The mark of mystery, as distinct from these, is that it has a bearing on our life. It arises out of our experience and we are forced to deal with it. But we deal with it by attitude and action, not by mere accumulation of knowledge nor exercise of the intellect. To degrade a mystery thus into a problem is to falsify it. We are given an apparent intellectual satisfaction, but we miss an opportunity for growth.

Through Mystery to Fidelity

Two illustrations may make the distinction clearer. Do not many of the discussions of freedom turn upon treating as a problem what is essentially a mystery? Thus, we begin by breaking up the self into various parts, temperament and disposition, character, motives, will, and so on. Then we set these various factors in operation and watch the result. The character, we say, determines the actions, or the will follows the strongest motive. So we explain freedom as 'really' another case of two forces making impact upon a body at the same time, or a cause producing the corresponding effect. Or we try to defend freedom within these limits, and cannot do it. For freedom is not something we can analyse in this way; our freedom is what does the analysis! It can therefore never be included in it. We are trying to solve a problem with the most important factor left out. Freedom is what we ourselves are, what we are responsible for. The question we have to ask ourselves is not: Are we free? but: How shall we use our freedom?

Similarly, we speak of the problem of evil, but we should do better to employ the term mystery instead. For evil is most certainly not something outside us for which we have to find the appropriate place in some all-inclusive and all-harmonizing system. Evil is in its very nature inexplicable, for it is that which does not fit in, which ought not to be there at all. If it could be accounted for, it would not be evil. But it is something with which we have to live. We have no right, for example, to ask why God permits evil unless we also face the fact that we ourselves permit a great deal of evil to exist that it is in our power to sweep away. Nor

do we usually realize that the demand that evil should
be eliminated might well have serious consequences
for ourselves! My primary relation to evil is that I
should do something about it, whether by entering in
sympathy into the lot of those who suffer or by eradi-
cating evil wherever this is within my power. And as
far as moral evil is concerned, I can always reduce its
hold upon one part of the world—my own life.

We might cite many more instances in which this
distinction is a valid and a fruitful one. The existence of
God is a mystery; God is not to be demonstrated by
the intellect but to be apprehended by the total self.
Theology would gain immensely by the acceptance of
Marcel's distinction. The doctrine of predestination is a
clear instance of how a mystery is degraded when it is
treated as a problem. The deep sense of gratitude that
overwhelms a man when he realizes how much he
owes to conditions over which he has no control, to
what was given to him at birth, must not be rational-
ized into an explanation of how our diverse fortunes
come about by some divine decree. I suspect, too, that
the Athanasian Creed is the classic example of the con-
fusion of a mystery evoking awe and wonder with an
intellectual puzzle.

(c)

The next step forward in the argument can only be
taken when we understand that mystery and problem
are not two different categories in which various
experiences can be fitted. The same experience belongs

at one level to problems and at another to mysteries. We may take an illustration from Marcel. I am ill and send for the doctor. He examines me, diagnoses my complaint, and prescribes a course of treatment. I must remain in bed for a month. His attitude to the illness is a scientific one: it is a problem to be solved, and he goes on to the next patient and *his* problem, to deal with it in the same way. But when the door closes behind the doctor and I am left alone, the illness takes on a quite different colour. I have to live with it for a month, and that is a moral situation in which I must act as a responsible individual. Shall I be morose and exacting, fretting all the while on the work perforce left undone? Or shall I seek by every means in my power to lighten the burden for those who must wait on me during the next month? Shall I even resolve to use my illness as a heaven-sent opportunity for recollection, meditation, and undisturbed entry into the presence of God?

What has happened in the process thus described is a movement within experience effected by reflection thereon. Here we come to the distinction Marcel draws between primary and secondary reflection. While he owes much to Bergson and agrees with him that the intellect has a spatializing and therefore destructive effect, he refuses to identify life with mere spontaneity and as such liable to be impaired when thought is brought to bear upon it. He would say that thought is an integral part of life, one of the activities by which we live. What is important is that we do not arrest it half-way but carry it right through.

Through Mystery to Fidelity

The first application of reflection to experience is apt to be analytic merely, though this may be of the utmost value where we are dealing with something in the world of objects, with something that we have. If I am expecting a party of friends to dinner, I sit down to consider the tastes of each and decide how best to entertain them. If a society suffers from extremes of wealth and poverty, a responsible statesman will collect statistics and plan how to eliminate such injustice. In each case, there is a problem to be solved and, once the appropriate technique and the necessary knowledge have been found, the solution is in sight. But where something personal is at stake, the situation is different. There the tendency of primary reflection will be, as we have already seen, to turn a mystery into a problem and so to falsify it altogether. What is necessary is to carry reflection further, penetrating by hint and metaphor and symbol into a realm in which we participate and which we do not merely survey. So we can hope to reconstruct and to envisage as a whole what had previously been broken up. Our thinking thus transcends the object knowledge of common sense and science, but it remains within experience all the while. The transcendent is not anything that lies beyond experience, it is its depth, its ultimate reference.

We may perhaps follow Marcel best on this point by considering two illustrations he employs. First, we ask the question: What is the relation between my body and myself? Primary reflection treats this as a problem, and it distinguishes between the body I have and

160

myself as the possessor of this. But when I examine
what is meant by this body, I find that it is *a* body and
not *my* body. The account science gives of the body
is as applicable to yours as to mine: it is just what is
described in any text-book of anatomy or physiology.
Clearly, we must go on beyond this. Common-sense
would say that I 'have' my body. But what is meant by
that? I have an opinion, a piano, a dog, a family: do I
have a body in the same sense as one of these? If so,
which of them? Is it not rather the case that my body is
the original instance of having and all the rest are but
derived from this and partially representative of it?

'*Within* every ownership, every kind of ownership I
exercise, there is this kernel that I feel to be there at
the centre; and this kernel is nothing other than the
experience—an experience which of its very nature
cannot be formulated in intellectual terms—by which
my body is mine.'[1]

Paradoxically, we may say that I only *have* my body
in so far as I *am* my body, that is, in so far as I do not
separate it from myself. Of course, there are occasions
when this is precisely what I do. I look at my body as
something over which I must exercise control, which
I must not pamper as I have been doing, I force it to
go on when, as we say, it demands to rest. Yet in
controlling it I control myself.

'It is in so far as I enter into some kind of relationship (though relationship is not an adequate term for
what I have in mind) with the body, some kind of
relationship which resists being made wholly objective

[1] *The Mystery of Being*, I, 97.

Through Mystery to Fidelity

to the mind, that I can properly assert that I am identical with my body.'[1]

My relation to my body is therefore unique and indefinable. It is in feeling rather than in thought; my relation to it is a mode of participation that transcends all the distinctions we usually employ between external and internal, between activity and passivity. Here again we must be on our guard against assimilating participation to sharing in objects. We come nearest to it if we consider the nature of love as participation in the life of another without either destroying his individuality or maintaining him as an object.

To return for a moment to the relation between the self and its body. What we have seen reveals to us the fundamental human situation as one of incarnation. I am involved in, I participate in, the world, I can think only within and out of concrete situations. That is of the utmost importance for philosophy. It means that the philosopher may not abstract from the historical situation in which he is set and concentrate on timeless problems such as those of language and its analysis. He is embedded in a society and a civilization for which he has a share of responsibility and all his work must be done against this background.

The second illustration of the difference between the two types of reflection turns on the question: What is my life? How am I related to my life? It might be suggested that my life is all the events that make up my past, it is a story that can be told and that I myself can tell. Or that it is what I have so far accomplished. But

---

[1] *Ibid.*, 101.

any such account of my life would cut it off from the present in which I actually live, would make it something I have or had rather than what I am. The final import of my life is seen when I find in it the same mysterious relationship that obtains between myself and my body. I can regard my life as something I have, in which case I can come to the decision to throw it away. By so doing I devalue it entirely, I reduce it to the status of a thing. I declare it mine only in the sense in which, say, a worn-out suit is that I send to the jumble sale. On the other hand, I may sacrifice my life at the call of duty; in which case, paradoxically, the act by which I give away my life is the one by which I affirm it most fully. A man is never more truly himself than in a moment of high dedication; he feels then that at last he is living truly and without qualifica tion. It is as if he were responding to a call that comes at once from within him and from beyond him. Here again we are in the realm of participation. The meaning of our life, we may say, does not lie on the surface but in the depths. We are most fully ourselves as we transcend ourselves; we only are as we acknowledge that we have been given to ourselves; my being is not a fact but a vocation.

(d)

So we arrive at the most urgent and the most perplexing of all questions: Who am I? I may be asked the question: 'Who are you?' perhaps by a stranger, but more probably by an official who is waiting to enter on a form the particulars I give him. Name, age, income, profession, family—he appears to be satisfied with this information. But am I? Do I not feel that in this investigation my essential self has been overlooked, that what I am is rather what does not enter into this inventory than what does? Hence I am faced by the question: Who am I? Anyone who has really endeavoured to answer this question knows how far it may take him. When one analyses one's motives, what problems arise! Is the account I give of myself a reliable one, or is it another device to evade the agony of full self-knowledge? I endeavour to be sincere, but how do I know when I am sincere? Where is the reality and where the pretence?[1]

There is, of course, an easy way of dealing with this question. It is to falsify it at the outset by treating it as though it were concerned, not with a person, but with a thing. We are constantly doing that in our relations with others: we analyse and explain them, we classify and dissect. We treat them as fixed quantities, as given natures, so that we imagine we can predict in advance what they will do. In our ignorance we create a role they are to fill, and we go on to identify them with this role. Then, just when we least expect it, they shatter the role, reveal themselves in some new and disconcerting light, and force us to change ourselves if we are to do justice to them. In much the same way, we act where we should live; we play a part before the

---

[1] Several paragraphs in this section are reproduced (with permission) from my article on 'Gabriel Marcel, A Theatre of Sincerity' in *The Contemporary Review* for February, 1952.

world, lose ourselves in our social function, anything
to save ourselves from the need to face challenging
situations and to give and receive freely in our relations
with others. But life does not allow of this false security; it is unpredictable and forces upon us the sharp
and painful effort to recover our lost authenticity.

This quest for sincerity, for the discovery of the real
self, is something to the presentation of which the
drama lends itself better than any other medium. Again
and again, therefore, Marcel as dramatist shows us
human beings like ourselves attempting to avoid the
pain and exposure of self-knowledge, but unable to do
so. They are engaged in something much more exacting than self-analysis; for the self with which they are
faced is one that needs not merely to be known, it
needs to be changed in some drastic fashion, and the
play shows them wrestling with the question whether
they are willing for this conversion, this transformation
that will redeem. Often Marcel leaves them at this
point; he does not tell us the decision at which they
arrive. To do so would militate against his purpose,
for the spectator of his drama is also involved in it.
He too is challenged to self-knowledge, not merely
entertained by an intriguing problem skilfully presented on the stage.

In some respects, the simplest and most moving of
the plays that have this as their theme is *Un Homme de
Dieu* (1925). The play opens in the home of a Protestant
pastor in Paris, Claude Lemoyne by name. Years before, when they were in a country parish, his wife
Edmée had been unfaithful with Michel Sandier. On

her confession, though after a soul-crisis so acute that he even contemplated abandoning his vocation, he forgave her and accepted Michel's child as his own daughter. Now Sandier is in Paris, mortally ill, and longing to see his child before he dies. The wife would refuse the request indignantly, but the husband insists on granting it. His conduct and Sandier's insinuations in the interview that follows evoke in her a doubt that shakes her confidence both in her husband and in herself. Was his forgiveness of her genuine? Did he pardon as a man or as a minister? Had he ever really cared for her, as man for woman? If he had, he would never have allowed the man who betrayed him to cross his threshold. And was her confession a real confession? Did she only make it because she was sure in advance of his response, so that to feign contrition was easy in comparison with the alternative, leaving him for her lover?

She reveals her doubts to her husband. He in his turn is reduced to despair. Have his actions all along been inauthentic, determined by what would keep up appearances, or, at best, what he felt was demanded of him by his position? Has he been acting a part throughout, never really being himself? He tells his daughter the whole story, and she too spurns a faith and virtue that may only be the uniform, as it were, of his profession. 'Who am I?' he cries in agony, as one support after another is taken from him even while, ironically enough, evidence accumulates of the esteem in which he is held by those who see nothing of what is taking place either in his home or in his heart. He wishes for death. 'It is man's one chance—even if it is not a door that opens for him. *To be known as one is, and then to sleep.*' Who can know us as we are? Only God. He had learned that before, and now he turns again to this hope. Alas, the play ends without a break-through to his real self. In the last scene, he and his wife are shown keeping up appearances to the end.

It would be gravely to misunderstand such a play to read it as an appeal for limitless self-scrutiny. We are meant rather to carry self-examination to the point at which it becomes clear to us how the self must be not only known but also changed, to turn from man's judgment and our own upon ourselves to the judgment of God. We are to commit ourselves to 'one who can only be described as an absolute Thou, a last and supreme resource for the troubled human spirit'.[1]

In *Le Monde Cassé* (1933) we are given a vivid picture of Paris society in the inter-war period. The central figure is Christiane Chesnaye, in whose life there is a hidden anguish she endeavours to conceal beneath a show of frivolity. She married Laurent, an efficient but undistinguished civil servant, in disappointment when the young man to whom she was passionately attached declared his intention of entering a monastery. In a striking passage, she confesses that there is that within her which protests against the life she leads, so that sometimes, if only for a few seconds, she yearns for a higher world than this broken and worthless one in which she plays apparently so brilliant a part. She is in search of her soul, but cannot find it. Nor can anyone

[1] *The Mystery of Being*, I, 152.

in her environment help her to it. Her husband cannot, with his cold, disdainful attitude. Nor can her admirers, though for a moment she is on the point of yielding.

Who then can bring her to her soul? Dom Maurice, the young Benedictine, is able to do it. He dies, and the news plunges Christiane almost into despair. Then the dead man's sister comes and brings further news of him. Evidence found after his death makes it clear that a realization had come to him, perhaps by a dream or a vision, of what his entry into the monastery must have cost her. Had his salvation perhaps been her perdition? From that moment, he felt for her 'a mysterious responsibility, yes, something like a spiritual paternity'. The relation between them was transfigured by being offered to God, and he prayed that she might enter into the transfiguration. After a momentary struggle, the news releases what was suppressed in her, and she turns to her husband with an invitation to unreserved fellowship. 'Ah!' he says, as he accepts the offer, 'it is as if you have been given back to me from the dead.' That indeed is what has happened. Self-knowledge has led to self-transformation, to conversion by surrender to the higher world in which she had hitherto been but a rare visitant. To know oneself, one must die and be born again.

(e)

It is clear that this self-knowledge is not arrived at by introspection only. It is ethical and not merely psychological. It is knowledge of oneself in certain concrete relations to other selves. But what are other persons? We may add here to the distinctions already established between problem and mystery, having and being, another of the same order, that between object and presence.

We are apt to suppose that to be present with a person means to be in his neighbourhood, to occupy space and time along with him. But in this way we assimilate the relation between persons to a mere juxtaposition between things. In what sense is the person who sleeps during a lecture present at it? In what sense am I present for a person who unveils his deepest need to me while all the time I am preoccupied, my thoughts elsewhere? What is meant by such expressions as 'absence of mind' and 'presence of mind'? Are they not pointers to some deeper understanding of presence?

I sit in the same room with a person, even speak to him, but all our intercourse is purely formal. No influence passes from the one to the other, each remains afterwards what he was before; there is communication without communion. But another person enters the room and, as we say, he makes his presence felt at once; what follows is a vital experience from which I emerge refreshed. 'When somebody's presence does really make itself felt, it can refresh my inner being; it reveals me to myself, it makes me more fully myself than I should be if I were not exposed to its impact.'[1] We may take Marcel's own instance of the woman who has charm. There is an atmosphere about

[1] *Ibid.*, 205.

169

her, a radiance that remains long after she has left the room. 'A presence is a reality; it is a kind of influx, it depends upon us to be permeable to this influx, but not, to tell the truth, to call it forth.'[1]

There are three notions that fall to be considered here. (*a*) The first is that of *intersubjectivity*, the relation between persons as opposed to that between things or that of a person to a thing. Here Marcel employs the language with which Martin Buber has familiarized us and opposes an I-Thou to an I-It relation. The other person represents a call to me and upon me; I become myself in such measure as I respond. We do not infer the existence of other persons from that of objects that are, presumably, animated like ourselves. The knowledge of other selves is given in and with the knowledge of ourselves and *vice versa*. Intersubjectivity is primary, we participate in one another before we are able to study and to manipulate one another. This participation, as in the case of the body, must not be understood in any spatial sense. Persons are not mutually exclusive, nor are they mutually inclusive. Our relations to each other are external only in so far as they are assimilated to that between objects; in mutual understanding, above all, in love we transcend the distinction between external and internal. We transcend equally that between giving and receiving. Did not John Stuart Mill, for example, say of his wife that it was not possible to distinguish in his work what was due to himself and what to her? In such a relationship, we receive from the other what is at the same time

[1] *The Philosophy of Existence*, 24.

most intimately our own. Such love is the fulfilment of intersubjectivity, in it we know even as we ourselves also are known.

(*b*) The second is *availability*. If I speak to a person, he is only present in so far as he holds himself in readiness to hear what I have to say, is open to me and available to help me.

'The person who is at my disposal is the one who is capable of being with me with the whole of himself when I am in need: while the one who is not at my disposal seems merely to offer me a temporary loan raised on his resources. For the one I am a presence; for the other I am an object.'[1]

(*c*) The third is *fidelity*. Man, as Nietzsche put it, is the only animal capable of making a promise. He can commit the future, bind himself now to what he will do in a year's time. But what right has anyone to do that? Can we control what we shall become, what our mood will be when the time comes to implement our promise? Today, while full of sympathy, I promise to call and see my sick friend again in a week's time. When next week comes I am busy and feel no particular sympathy: why then should I go and see him? Is it because of the general principle that one should keep one's word? Perhaps. Yet such a principle is so general that it must admit of exceptions, and may not this be one? There is no doubt something of fidelity to myself involved, for I should feel ashamed of myself if I did not

---

[1] *Ibid.*, 26. It is perhaps worth remarking that this presentation of availability as the key to presence seems to offer the possibility of an interpretation of the presence of Christ in the Eucharist superior to the traditional ones.

go. I regard self-consistency as a virtue. Yet not absolutely so, since otherwise the conversion for which we have been pleading would be ruled out. And to what self should I be faithful? To the one that made the promise or to the one that I am now? There is clearly no obligation on me to be faithful to the self of the passing moment and its emotions. Is there then a permanent self that lays claim to my fidelity? Such a self will lie deeper than that of every day. But where is it to be located? Where indeed but with God? In the last resort, as we have said before, what I am is less a fact than a vocation. Fidelity is therefore to God and to the self one is before him, since absolute fidelity is due to him alone.

But the self I am before God does not exist in any sort of isolation. The fact of intersubjectivity is fundamental. I am what I am in and through my relations with other persons. There is therefore fidelity to the other. This is not to be understood in any static sense, as though either I or the one to whom I am faithful were a fixed object to whom the same relation must always be maintained. Personal relations are an opportunity for mutual creation—or destruction. For we participate in each other and we make each other. That is true especially in the most intimate relationships of life. Those who enter on marriage must not think of themselves as continuing to be under new conditions what they were before. They will be called upon to grow into new selves, each indebted to the other for what he or she becomes. Only so will their life together be stable and fruitful in blessing. Love is an act of creative fidelity, in virtue of which each party to the relationship constitutes the other as presence and therefore to be held sacred. What this means for the question of death and immortality will be seen in the next section.

Fidelity to God, it follows from what has been said, is not something separate from and in addition to fidelity to oneself and to the other. It is achieved rather in and through these.

One more point. Intersubjectivity applies not only between selves but also within them. That it is possible to speak of fidelity to oneself suggests as much. Also what has been said of self-knowledge is an indication of how the self can be sincere or insincere in its relation to itself. The self can be at once I and Thou in a searching conversation and inquiry; I have been given to myself and I am responsible for myself. Self-dedication springs 'from the very depths of my own life'. Here again we reach the point at which the self is seen to be mystery, something much more than a problem.

(f)

We are now in a position to approach the central and final mystery, that of Being itself. What kind of ontology will Marcel give us? It is clear that it will not follow the traditional lines. It might seem, for example, that as each special science deals with its own selection of objects and reaches generalizations concerning these, so there would be room for an ultimate science, ontology, that would reach generalizations concerning that object which is present in all other objects, namely, Being. That would give us a problem, and, as we have seen again and again, the realm of problems is inhabited only by abstractions and partial truths. Or we might think of Being as the subject to which all objects are attached as predicates, or as the predicate of every subject. But either of these suggestions would draw it down to a level at which it would be classified, placed, and accounted for as another instance of something with which we are already familiar. We must find another way to our goal.

That goal is provided by the principle of incarnation. In other words, our inquiry must set out from the situation in which we find ourselves, not as thinkers only, but as persons. Our world is largely mechanized and depersonalized, its typical figure is the bureaucrat and its ever-present temptation is to reduce the individual to a social function, to identify what he is with what he is good for. Social intercourse takes the place of genuine communion, we touch but do not meet, talk but do not speak one to another. It is as if a veil is drawn over what we really are, as if all the world has become a stage on which we play our parts, the only spectators available being engaged equally in pretence and posturing. So there arises in the more sensitive among us a craving for what *is* as opposed to what seems to be or puts itself forward as being. This 'exigence of Being' is the root of philosophy today. All may not feel it, nevertheless those who feel it know that it is no private demand but something that is required if one is to be truly human. Being is therefore

174

to be found by following this inner demand whither it may lead.

To do this, we must distinguish clearly between existence and being. Here it is necessary to point out that Marcel does not use the word 'existence' in the sense in which it is employed by the other thinkers with whom this study is concerned. Existence for him is the primary datum of our experience, the starting-point of all thought, 'a massive assurance' that does not admit of proof or disproof, because these can be brought to bear only on particular instances of existence and never on existence as such. It is to be found first in the self. I exist, this is the indubitable certainty from which thinking sets out, 'the existential fulcrum', as Marcel terms it. But I exist, of course, not as any transcendental self or pure subject, but as incarnate, as in a particular situation along with others who are also incarnate. Nor is it possible to distinguish between existing and manifesting one's existence.

'Let me say that this impossibility of doubting one's own existence of which we have been talking seems to be linked to a kind of exclamatory awareness of oneself; this awareness is expressed in the small child (and, indeed, perhaps already at the level of consciousness of the higher animals) by cries, by leaps, and so on, though naturally with the adult its expression is more measured and restrained.'[1]

This existence is shared by things as well as by persons. For do not things have a mysterious power of

[1] *The Mystery of Being*, II, 91. On this whole subject see Chenu: *Le Théâtre de Gabriel Marcel*(1948), 57ff.

manifesting themselves to us, of impressing themselves upon us? We do not realize this because we live in a world full of machine-products; the natural object and the work of art command us as the radio set and the automobile cannot do. It would seem as though we must arrange what enters into our experience in a scale, with the minimum of being at the bottom and the maximum at the top. My cat *is* in a richer sense than the rug on which he lies and my friend again in a far richer sense than the cat. The exigence of being is a yearning for value, for fulness. To attain to being is to come home. 'There is always a gap between me and my being; I can narrow the gap, it is true, but at least in this life I cannot hope to bridge it.'[1] There is accordingly a depth of significance in the acknowledgment 'I am' that is not to be found in the mere manifestation of my existence.

'It should not be put forward in any defiant or presumptuous tone; rather should it be whispered humbly, with fear and wonder. I say *with humility*, because, after all, as we shall see more and more clearly, this being is something that can only be granted to us as a gift; it is a crude illusion to believe it is something which I can give to myself: *with fear*, because I cannot even be certain that I may not make myself unworthy of the gift, so unworthy that I should be condemned to losing it, did not grace come to my assistance: and finally *with wonder*, because this gift brings as its companion the light, because this gift *is light*.'[2]

It follows from this that being is in persons and is

[1] *Ibid.*, II, 31. [2] *Ibid.*, II, 32.

accessible only to love. The other person becomes for me a being only as I approach him with respect, as I regard him as a centre of freedom and responsibility existing in his own right. I only attain to being in myself as I adopt this attitude towards others. Being is in intersubjectivity, we participate in it as we share life with each other. The I-Thou relation, the fidelity of which we have spoken earlier—it is here that the mystery of being is open to us. It is not an object but a presence; we cannot account for it but we must take account of it. Finally, it is something we are free to accept or to refuse; we may choose to exist rather than to be; we may even degrade others who are persons to the level of things.

Being is open therefore to faith, hope, and love, and not accessible to any scientific knowledge or technique. We discern the other as sacred and imperishable and, so doing, we apprehend with awe that we ourselves are judged so by God. For all self-knowledge leads us to the self that is vocation rather than actuality, the self that comes to be just in such measure as we are willing to die and rise again. Fidelity to the other is grounded in fidelity to God; he is a mysterious being who has been entrusted to me and for whom I am responsible; he is accessible to me only as I abandon the will-to-power that would use him for the humble, grateful acceptance that allows him to be sacred in my eyes. My attitude is at once love and faith, for these are not to be distinguished finally. Faith is 'opening a credit to . . . rallying to . . . and such an attitude is possible only in relation to what is of the order of persons rather than of things'. I believe in God, therefore, when I hold myself at his disposal, pledge myself to him, live my life in his light. This relation to him lies beyond proof and disproof, for by it I participate, I do not merely know. This point is all important. My faith in God is not a mental condition of mine which may or may not be correlated with some object independent of it called God. My faith, hope, and love actually participate in the divine life, so that they are self-authenticating. That is to say, they carry their own evidence for me so long as I believe; when I suspend faith and examine it from outside (as in certain circumstances I must do) it then becomes a conviction with more or less probability attached to it.

The other person as sacred leads me to God. But love is the discernment of the other as imperishable, and this is the hope of immortality. The loved person is imperishable in two senses. He is of such a quality for me that he ought to endure, he possesses a unique worth that may not be dispensed with. And also his being as opposed to his existence moves in a realm exempt from change; it is not an object that it should cease to exist as the Roman Empire once existed but does so no longer. But it is precisely because the loved one is imperishable in these two senses that his death is so awful. For death reduces the person to the status of a thing, he goes the way of objects in the world, though his place is not with them; what ought not to perish appears to perish before my eyes. I therefore turn from death with the hope of immortality and stake out a claim for him in the beyond.

Through Mystery to Fidelity

So we arrive at a metaphysic of hope. What for the onlooker is a piece of wishful thinking is for the one who thus hopes grounded in reality. What he hopes for is not for the continuance of the other person as he might hope for the persistence of a flower that is withering. Because he participates by love in the being of the other person, he hopes that that participation will endure and conquer death. It is as if he said to the loved one:

'Whatever changes may intervene in what I see before me, you and I will persist as one: the event that has occurred, and which belongs to the order of accident, cannot nullify the promise of eternity which is enclosed in our love, in our mutual pledge.'[1]

Marcel speaks of this hope as a 'prophetic assurance'. It is of the same order, that is to say, as the confidence with which the political refugee from Eastern Europe declares that liberty in his country is indestructible, that no tyranny will ever crush it, or that with which the scientific worker addresses himself again and again to his task, never doubting that in the end he will see his way through. But an assurance of this nature has implications for conduct here and now. I do not genuinely hope in the indestructibility of the whole formed by myself and the person to whom I am attached if, at his death, I allow him to drop out of my thoughts, relegating him to the past. There must, it would seem, be a counterpart in my continuing life to my trust that the other will endure for ever. If the link between us is to remain, I must not simply appeal to

[1] *Ibid.*, 154f.

God to preserve it, I must do my best to preserve it myself. I must live with the memory of the one who has been taken from me so that he never becomes an object but always remains a presence, a centre of influence, of guidance, and of healing. As we prolong ourselves in others during life, so it is for us who survive to preserve whatever was of worth in the departed by taking it up into our own being. Our love should become an act of creative fidelity.

> When lofty thought
> Lifts a young heart above its mortal lair,
> And love and life contend in it, for what
> Shall be its earthly doom, the dead live there
> And move like winds of light on dark and stormy
> air.

That we live in hearts of those we leave behind is therefore not to be understood as a substitute for personal immortality, but as a necessary complement of it.

(g)

As we come now to the end of our journey, we are conscious that it has been a pilgrimage. We have travelled from atheist humanism to faith in God, from dread before death to the hope of life everlasting. Yet the goal we should reach was not determined from the beginning; there has been adventure in the enterprise, and the hazard of frightful loss. We set out for a shrine, but did not know whether, on arrival, we should find it empty or fraught with a divine presence. Now that we have worshipped before that presence, we do not forget the road by which we came to it. Such certitude of God as we have has been won by facing the awful possibility that he might not be. That we are persons and not things, that we are free and responsible, that we are not alone but with others, that our destiny is to transcend ourselves, that our fate is in our own hands —all this we knew at the outset. But whether we should find God in these things or miss him wholly—that we did not know. But now we find that our freedom is by his grace and our human love is rooted and grounded in his love.

Such an existentialism as that of Jaspers and Marcel is not a final philosophy. It does not aspire to a place among the systems, where Aristotle and Aquinas and Hegel are honoured. To be existential means to be concerned about our actual situation, and that not as something to be studied but as a state of affairs for which we are responsible. We are incarnate beings and we must think as such. The truth we win may well prove insufficient for those who come after us, but if by means of it we can meet God in our own day, we can be content. Yet it is not detached from the past. It is no revolt against the philosophical tradition. Rather does it seek to appropriate and live by this, by the personal insights and decisions that are veiled from us by, yet revealed to us in, the arguments of a Plato and a Kant.

But it in its turn must be appropriated personally. It is to be judged from within, by one who has taken seriously its contention that our philosophy is only our thinking because it was, before that, our decision. Two such decisions are required of us. The first is whether we are to count the world of objects that may be known and manipulated as the only real one or as the ante-chamber to one that is much more real. The second is how we enter that real world when we have found it, as those who would impose themselves upon its emptiness or as those who would receive its fulness into themselves.

'Man is a useless passion.' 'Man is a being who exists in relation to God.' The choice is finally between these two.

Index

Index

184

Index

3139